TITANIC

SINKS!

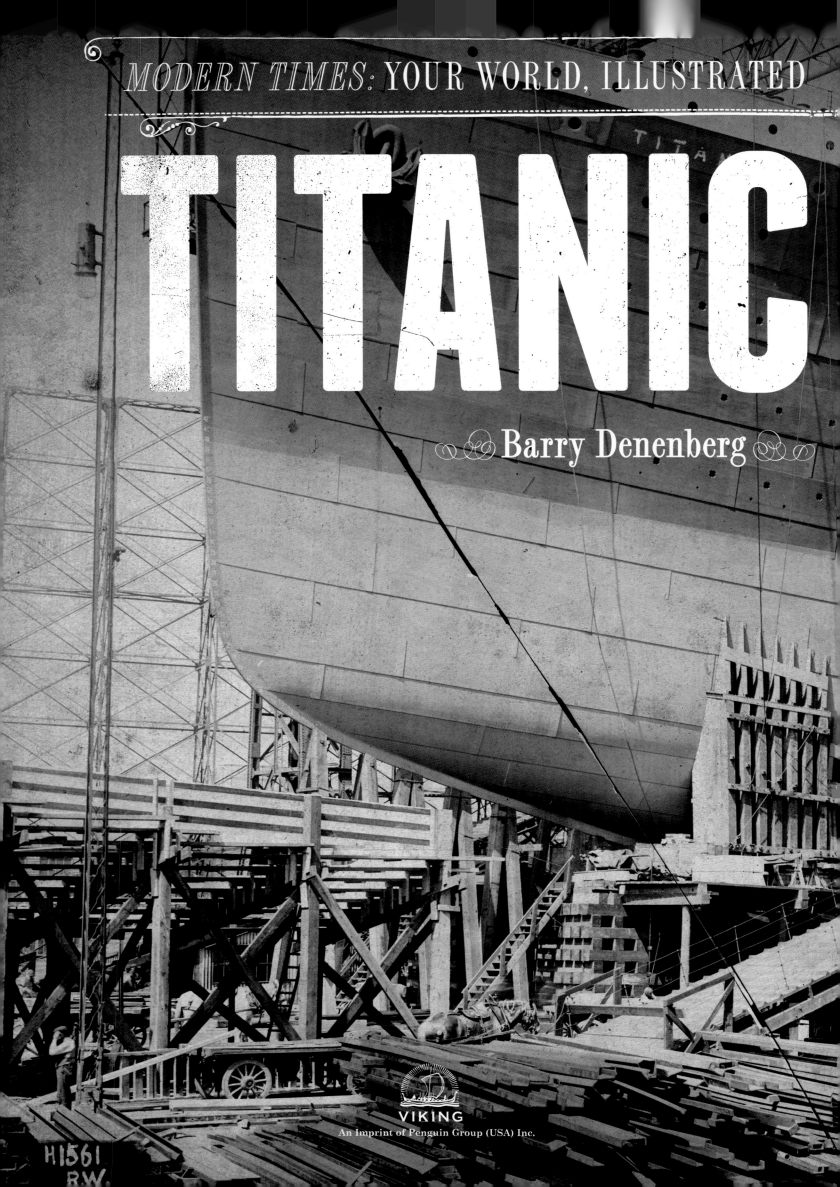

MODERN TIMES: YOUR WORLD, ILLUSTRATED

TITANIC

Barry Denenberg

VIKING
An Imprint of Penguin Group (USA) Inc.

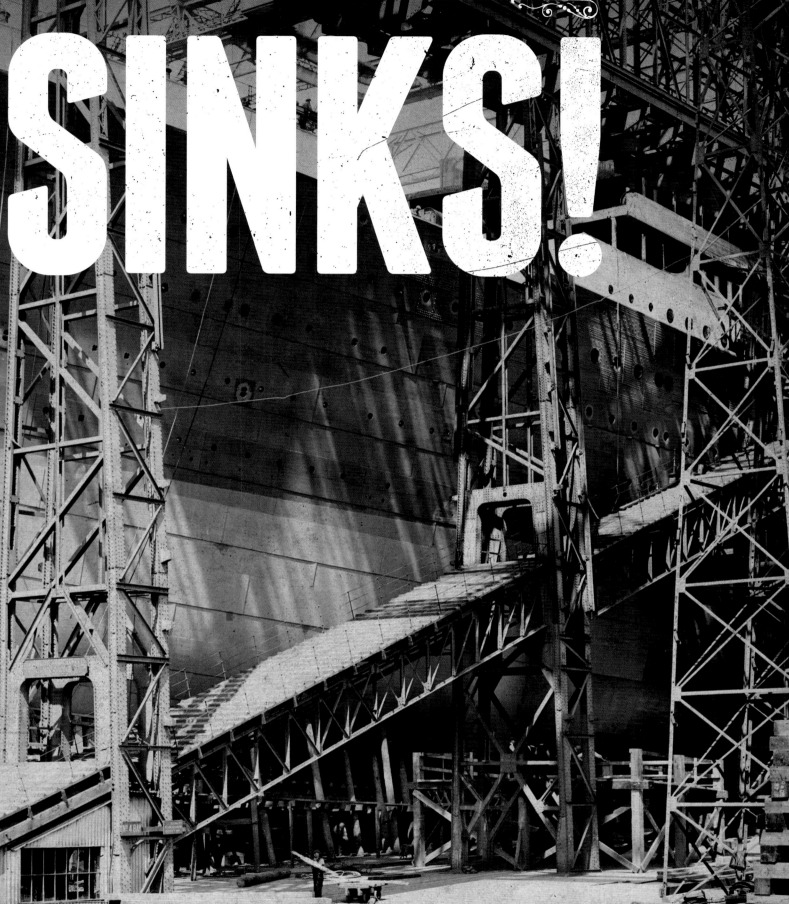

SINKS!

VIKING
Published by Penguin Group
Penguin Young Readers Group, 345 Hudson Street, New York, New York 10014, U.S.A.

Penguin Books Ltd, Registered Offices: 80 Strand, London WC2R 0RL, England

First published in 2011 by Viking, a division of Penguin Young Readers Group

1   3   5   7   9   10   8   6   4   2

Text copyright © Barry Denenberg, 2011
All rights reserved
"Desolation Row" by Bob Dylan, copyright © 1965 by Warner Bros. Inc.;
renewed 1993 by SPECIAL RIDER MUSIC. All rights reserved.
Photo credits appear on p. 69

LIBRARY OF CONGRESS CATALOGING-IN-PUBLICATION DATA
Denenberg, Barry.
Titanic sinks! / by Barry Denenberg.
p. cm.
ISBN 978-0-670-01243-5 (hardcover)
1. Titanic (Steamship)—Juvenile literature.
2. Shipwrecks—North Atlantic Ocean—Juvenile literature.
I. Title.
G530.T6D46 2011   910.9163'4—dc22   2011012040

Manufactured in China   Set in Caslon, Regula
BOOK DESIGN BY JIM HOOVER

For Jean and Emma

CONTENTS

• A LETTER FROM THE PUBLISHER •

MODERN TIMES MAGAZINE began publication in 1907, one year before plans for the largest (four city blocks long) and most luxurious ship in the world were announced. Our staff reported on every aspect of the *Titanic* story from day one. We now proudly present the very best of those articles in this special edition magazine, lavishly enhanced by selected photographs and illustrations.

The first pages set the scene: the intense four-year design and construction process; the much anticipated launch; the captain taking command; the ship's successful sea trials; and, finally, sailing day.

Next is the journal of our chief correspondent, S. F. Vanni, who accompanied the liner on her maiden voyage. Vanni's meticulous notes start as the *Titanic* leaves port and continues until the very last minutes of her tragically brief existence.

Following the journal, the harrowing hours in the lifeboats are relived by survivors, and the role of the rescue ship *Carpathia* is recounted.

Finally, "A Closing Note from the Publisher" brings the story to a close and provides some perspective.

TITANIC SINKS! is designed to allow you to experience the unprecedented no-expense-spared luxury of the *Titanic*; to meet the rich and famous in first class; to mingle with those down below in steerage; to sense that something terrible is happening; to realize that not only is there no time, there are not enough lifeboats; to see, hear, and feel the panic and confront the terrible choices the passengers did: heroism or cowardice? Dignity or survival? Life or death?

When you turn to the last page, we feel confident you will be able to grapple with the questions surrounding the greatest peacetime disaster of the twentieth century; questions that have persisted for a hundred years:

*Did arrogance and corporate greed doom the *Titanic*?

*Was the captain racing to New York, despite warnings that there were icebergs dead ahead?

*Why didn't the lookouts see the "berg" in time?

*Why did most of the lifeboats leave half empty?

*Was the rule "women and children" first followed?

*Why did so many third-class passengers perish while so many crewmen survived?

The sinking of the *Titanic* was, for that generation of Americans, what Pearl Harbor, the Kennedy assassination, and 9/11 were for later ones. It marked a turning point: before it life was one way, and after it, well, after it nothing was ever the same.

Author Helen Candee, an astute observer and *Titanic* survivor described the night the *Titanic* sank as "a fancy-dress ball in Dante's Hell."

Welcome aboard.

Mary Hudson
Publisher
Modern Times: Your World, Illustrated

WHITE STAR NAMES NEW LUXURY LINER *TITANIC*

Harland and Wolff director Lord William James Pirrie (left) and White Star's chairman, J. Bruce Ismay.

PIRRIE AND ISMAY DISCUSS CONCEPT OVER HAVANAS AND BRANDY

MONDAY, APRIL 27, 1908

A spokesman for the White Star Line, the British steamship company owned, since 1902, by the vast shipping combine formed by American financier J. P. Morgan, announced Wednesday, April 22, that one of its two new 45,000-ton luxury liners would be named *Titanic*.

The ambitious project was initiated at the London residence of Lord William James Pirrie, controlling director of premier shipbuilder Harland and Wolff. Pirrie discussed the concept over Havana cigars and Napoleon brandy with White Star's chairman and son of the company founder, J. Bruce Ismay (this, after the ladies had kindly departed).

"LUXURY AND COMFORT— NOT SPEED" GOAL "LAST WORD IN MARINE CONSTRUCTION"

J. Pierpont Morgan, American financier and director of IMM, the trust that owns White Star.

The two titans of the shipping industry made some preliminary sketches and considered long-range financial forecasts for the daunting undertaking. It will take an estimated three years to build.

It is believed that the discussions were prompted by last year's much acclaimed maiden voyages of White Star's arch rival Cunard's two ships—*Lusitania* and *Mauretania*—acknowledged to be today's fastest and finest passenger ships. A White Star official stated emphatically that "Luxury and comfort—not speed" were their goal (alluding to the Cunard's speed, which is considered by experts to be unsurpassable). The official went on to say that "British know-how backed by American capital will prove to be an unbeatable combination."

Like all White Star ships, *Titanic* and her older sister, *Olympic* (a third, *Gigantic*, is only in the planning stage), will be built at Harland and Wolff's Belfast, Ireland, shipyard, which will be radically altered to accommodate the two huge vessels. Both principles stated that there were currently no docks large enough for the two behemoths.

A Harland and Wolff spokesman added that "As always, superior quality in every aspect of shipbuilding is our primary concern, and no expense will be spared to create luxury liners that are without peer and that represent the last word in marine construction."

"SUPERIOR QUALITY IN EVERY ASPECT OF SHIPBUILDING IS OUR PRIMARY CONCERN"

FIFTEEN-YEAR-OLD DIES IN FALL FROM *TITANIC'S* HULL

14,000 TO BUILD BEHEMOTHS

Monday, April 25, 1910

Virtually all of Harland and Wolff's 14,000 employees—from architects, draftsmen, and interior designers to electricians and riveters—have been committed to the shipbuilder's ambitious project. The two ships, *Olympic* and *Titanic*, will be the largest vessels sailing the high seas and are being built side-by-side simultaneously.

The ambitious construction project involves, among other things, the installation of three million rivets in each ship. Although the keel and the frame are being riveted hydraulically, the shell plating is being done (mostly) manually, and hand riveting is considered a rather difficult process. "Heater boys" hold the rivets at arm's length in tongs, heating them in the coke brazier that they keep cooking by pumping the stove bellows with their feet, making sure the rivets are heated to just the right "cherry red" temperature (too cold or too hot could mean an improper fit which could lead to problems along the seams). The rivets are then thrown to the "catch boys" who, after deftly cradling them in a wooden bowl, place each one in a hole overlapping the two plates. Another man then holds the plates while the "basher," wielding a heavy hammer beats the rivet until it is secure.

The arduous labor is performed by crews of four who are paid by the rivet, working nine-hour shifts in frigid cold and accompanied constantly by deafening noise.

THREE MILLION RIVETS TO BE USED

LARGEST VESSELS SAILING THE HIGH SEAS

The riveting squads are encouraged by Harland and Wolff's management team to work in a manner that combines precision and speed. Precision because proper workmanship is a must: improperly fitted hull plates could result in trouble later on the high seas. Speed because the more rapidly the riveting process moves along the sooner the *Titanic* will set sail on her maiden voyage.

Clearly this can be a daunting and dangerous job. Sadly this past week Samuel Joseph Scott, a fifteen-year-old "catch boy," fell from the *Titanic's* eleven-story-high hull and died.

Titanic's rudder, which will be used to steer the ship when in motion.
It is 78'8" high and 15'3" wide and weighs 101 1/4 tons. Workers are fitting the starboard tail shaft.

TITANIC'S VITAL STATISTICS

DESIGN PROCESS BEGINS—April 30, 1907
KEEL LAID—March 31, 1909
PROJECTED LAUNCH—May 31, 1911
SEA TRIALS BEGIN—April 2, 1912
MAIDEN VOYAGE—April 10, 1912

GROSS REGISTERED TONNAGE—46,328
LENGTH—882 feet, 9 inches
WIDTH—92 feet
HEIGHT—175 feet
MAIN ENGINE SIZES—(2) 15,000 horsepower
(1) 16,000 horsepower
NUMBER OF BOILERS—24 double-ended
5 single-ended

NUMBER OF FURNACES—159
RUDDER WEIGHT—101.25 tons
ANCHOR WEIGHT—(3) 15.5 tons each
PROPELLER WEIGHTS—center, 22 tons;
(2) wing propellers, 38 tons each

LARGEST WHISTLE EVER MADE

FOUR FUNNELS—24 feet 6 inches diameter

NUMBER OF LIFEBOATS—16

NUMBER OF COLLAPSIBLE BOATS—4

COST—7.5 million dollars

★ ★

TITANIC LAUNCH DAZZLING SUCCESS!

LARGEST MAN-MADE MOVING OBJECT ON EARTH

★ ★

≈ A TRUE MARVEL OF THE AGE! ≈

Monday, June 12, 1911

The largest man-made moving object on earth, the White Star Line's *Titanic*, was launched at 12:13 Wednesday, May 31, 1911, from Harland and Wolff's slip #3 in Belfast, Ireland. She was released from the gantry that was especially built for the task of constructing the twentieth century's finest vessel—a true marvel of our age.

Officials from both White Star and Harland and Wolff boasted that the technologically advanced luxury liner would be able to survive all that man or nature could conjure up. Her sixteen watertight compartments (which the captain can close instantly merely by flipping a switch) would allow her to remain afloat long enough for the passengers and crew to be rescued in the extremely unlikely event that any-

thing happened to her. This feature, along with many other innovations in design and safety, render the exquisite new steamship "practically unsinkable" according to the leading industry magazine, *Shipbuilder*.

A White Star spokesman declared that

CAN SURVIVE ANYTHING; "PRACTICALLY UNSINKABLE"

the *Titanic* was "a technological miracle that was a testimony to the ongoing progress of mankind and the ability of science to overcome nature."

RIGHT: The *Titanic* at rest, shortly after launch. She was halted by drag chains and special anchors and then towed back to the shipyard by five tugs.

As is customary with all Harland and Wolff launchings, there was no christening and therefore no champagne. However, due to the great expectations associated with the event, three grandstands were set up to

WOMEN WAVE AS TUGS BLOW WHISTLES

accommodate dignitaries, spectators, and members of the press.

The *Titanic*'s movement began when hydraulic valves were opened and the restraining timbers supporting her were knocked away. Her 772 foot, 62-second-long trip down to the water was eased by 23 tons

TESTIMONY OF THE ONGOING PROGRESS OF MANKIND

of tallow, oil, and soft soap. Spectators and dockworkers cheered, women waved handkerchiefs, and tugs blew their whistles in salute.

Sadly, one of the workers, James Dobbins, 43, had his legs crushed during the launch when some of the wood shoring collapsed. Although he was rushed by ambulance to Royal Victoria hospital and operated on, he died two days later from contusions and shock. Dobbins is one of eight men who died building the *Titanic*.

THE TITANIC LAUNCHED

41569-
R.W.

Captain Edward John Smith posing for a picture
on the boat deck of the *Titanic*.

CAPTAIN SMITH TAKES COMMAND OF THE *TITANIC*

KNOWN AS "THE MILLIONAIRE'S CAPTAIN"

MONDAY, APRIL 1, 1912

On Monday, Captain Edward John "E. J." Smith took over command of White Star's *Titanic* in preparation for the colossal luxury liner's April 10 departure from Southampton, England, for New York City.

The captain, who is married and has

RADIATES CONFIDENCE

a fourteen-year-old daughter, looks the part, with his distinctive, closely trimmed white beard and ready smile. He is universally respected for his calm, responsible demeanor and take-charge manner. He is a favorite among seamen as well as the well-heeled travelers who have crossed the ocean with him many times. Smith is known as "the Millionaire's Captain" by the wealthy veteran travelers who routinely request berths on ships under his command. This has allowed him to command a salary that is twice as high as any other captain sailing today.

Smith, sixty-two, has served with White Star for the past thirty-two years—twenty-five of them as captain of seventeen ships.

Captain Smith's wife, Eleanor, and their daughter circa 1900.

According to some estimates he has logged two million miles during his illustrious career.

Smith, who radiates confidence, recently commented on modern-day sea travel, saying, "I cannot imagine any condition which would cause a ship to flounder. . . . Modern shipping has gone beyond that."

CHIEF OFFICER WILLIAM M. MURDOCH AND FIRST OFFICER CHARLES H. LIGHTOLLER JOIN CAPTAIN SMITH

Lightoller (right) and Murdoch preparing to close the gangway door.

Captain Smith has his critics, however. At the age of sixty-two he is near retirement (the *Titanic* is likely to be his last ship) and some suggest he might be too old. In addition, he was in command during three previous accidents. The most serious and most controversial, in September of last year, involved the *Titanic's* sister ship, the *Olympic*.

The *Olympic* had departed Southampton (from which the *Titanic* will leave) and was running parallel to the considerably smaller *Hawke*. The *Hawke* was sucked into the larger ship's hull by the wake she created. Thankfully there were no injuries, but unfortunately repairs were required. The *Olympic* was eventually taken back to Belfast and her voyage was cancelled. *Titanic's* maiden voyage was originally scheduled for March 20. After the accident at Harland and Wolff's shipyard, workmen were pulled off the *Titanic,* thereby necessitating that her departure date be postponed. The new date for the *Titanic's* eagerly anticipated maiden voyage is April 10, 1912.

An inquiry found that Captain Smith was responsible for the collision. The report concluded that he had difficulty adjusting to the huge proportions and attendant maneuvering problems of the *Olympic.*

There is some speculation that the collision between the *Olympic* and the *Hawke* is proof that these new, colossal vessels are simply too big for anyone to handle.

Joining him on the *Titanic* is Chief Officer William McMaster Murdoch and First Officer Charles Herbert Lightoller.

Mr. Murdoch is an affable Scotsman from a seagoing family. He is experienced (First Officer on the *Olympic*) and conscientious, with a well-earned reputation for steady nerves and good judgment under pressure. First Officer Lightoller has already led an adventurous life. He happily went off to sea as a young lad of thirteen, was shipwrecked four times since, and has survived a fire at sea (sometime later assuring his concerned sister: "Don't you bother, the sea is not wet enough to drown me. I'll never be drowned").

Lightoller has also managed somehow to find time to prospect for gold in the Yukon and ride the range as a cowboy in Canada. He joined White Star in 1900 and has served under Captain Smith numerous times, most recently on the *Oceanic*.

"QUEEN OF THE SEAS"

AN EXCLUSIVE MODERN TIMES LOOK AT THE TITANIC

MONDAY, APRIL 8, 1912

MODERN TIMES has just returned from Belfast, Ireland, where we had an exclusive eye-opening guided tour of White Star's new star attraction, the most aptly named *Titanic*. She left Belfast on April 2 and arrived in Southampton, England, shortly after midnight on April 4, having successfully completed her sea trials.

The *Titanic*'s equipment—turbines, engines, boilers, and propellers—was tested as the ship performed different maneuvers, including achieving top speed, slowing down, and stopping—all this while the recently assembled crew became familiar with their new, temporary home. Of course, all necessary adjustments were duly noted.

The *Titanic*'s reciprocating engines being constructed. Various parts are laid out on the shop floor.

Southampton is known as the "gateway to the world" and has been one of England's premier ports for two thousand years. The *Titanic* is scheduled to depart Southampton on April 10 for New York City, after stops at Cherbourg, France, and Queensland, Ireland.

One word of warning: stay close. It is so easy to lose your way on this sea-going city that White Star provides passengers with a guide book to help them negotiate the complex maze of corridors and commonways that crisscross the ship. (They also provide a most handy first- and second-class passenger list.)

We begin our tour in third class, located on the lowest section of the ship. Any-

one imagining "huddled masses yearning to breathe free" will, however, be sorely disappointed. The days of the dangerous ocean voyage to a new life in America are long gone. Today's vigorous competition for the "steerage" class business has resulted in a safer, infinitely more comfortable and affordable ocean crossing for all. It is well known in the steamship circles that the first-class passenger provides the publicity, but third class foots the bill. 955,000 emigrants are expected to disembark in New York this year alone.

The third-class area is clean, well-ventilated, and nicely lit. The spartan dining room's white walls are cheerfully relieved by

Third-class passengers on the *Titanic*'s forward well deck (tugs *Hector* and *Neptune* to the right).

A poster advertising the return trip departing from New York.

colorful, framed White Star posters, and the food served is plain but plentiful. Third-class passengers are called to meals via a gong, and have their own bakery. Breakfast choices are: oatmeal, smoked herring, tripe, onions, etc. There's a general room with a piano (there are five on board) and a smoking room. The small but comfortable sleeping closets have two to eight berths each for families traveling together. Naturally single

men and women are separated: men in the bow and women in the stern. The same occurs in the dining saloon: single men in one room and ladies and families in another.

Third-class passengers will be closely scrutinized by medical personnel before boarding because of America's strict immigration laws. In addition White Star's regulations state that any passengers who are diseased or "lunatic, idiot, deaf, dumb, blind, maimed, infirm, or above the age of sixty years, any woman without a husband with a child or children" or any person unable to care for himself without becoming a "public charge" will not be permitted entry. Officials assured us they expect this process to be smooth and orderly.

American law also requires that there be locked barricades (such as doors and gates) between third class and other passengers. This is merely a precaution, as no one wants any diseases to spread.

The second-class dining saloon (capacity 394) has long tables and chairs that swivel, and shares a galley with the first class. We stole a glance at the lunch menu, which features spaghetti au gratin, corned beef, roast mutton, ox tongue, and a very nice selection of desserts. In addition, there's a lounge area and a smoking room whose dark green Moroccan leather chairs remind us of our favorite New York and London clubs. Sleeping accommodations in second class are on a par with first-class rooms in any of today's better hotels (as is the cost of a ticket).

To emerge into the rarified air of the first-class section of the *Titanic* is to enter an atmosphere of unsurpassed lavishness and unparalleled opulence. One takes the magnificent grand staircase to the First Class Dining Saloon on D deck (unless you prefer to take one of the new electric lifts that provide such a valuable service to elderly passengers—there are three in first class and one in second).

The first-class dining saloon is the largest room afloat (92 feet by 114 feet—capacity 554), and we were immediately dazzled not only by its sheer immensity but by the glistening crystal goblets, shining silverware, and pristine china plates that floated on an ocean of crispy clean, snow-white tablecloths. The rim of the table, which is called a "fiddle," can be raised in the event of stormy weather. This prevents the dishes and glasses from sliding into your lap.

The elaborate, multi-course dinner is included in the price of the ticket; children, however, cannot eat in the first-class dining saloon unless full fare has been paid. The meal rivals those served in the finest restaurants on the continent. Dress is formal,

except for the last night to make allowances for packing one's things. We were allowed a glance at the menu planned for April 14 and were quite impressed.

There are sixty chefs and a kitchen support staff of thirty-six, including roast, fish, pasta, soup, and sauce cooks, bakers, and a cook who is solely responsible for preparing kosher meals. The galley is quite up-to-date with electric appliances, an ice-making machine, separate refrigerated rooms for meat, poultry, fish, vegetables, and eggs, and a wine and champagne refrigeration system that maintains bottles at the perfect temperature.

Adjoining the forward end of the dining saloon is a reception room where passengers can either meet before dinner or linger over coffee after, while listening to the ship's

Two of the cooks in the 60-by-92-foot combined first- and second-class galley.

The *Titanic's* first-class dining saloon. It can accommodate 554 diners, and formal attire is required.

orchestra. There are eight musicians and they play in various configurations—trio, quintet, and so on.

For those who prefer their dining more au courant there's the très fashionable à la carte restaurant, which has the benefit of allowing you to order what you want when you want. It's open throughout the day and is available for private dinner parties. Many are glad to avoid the endless menu in the first-class dining saloon, and this new kind of dining has been well received.

First class on the *Titanic* means an astonishing number of public rooms that are designed to suit the many and any moods of even the most discerning and demanding ocean-going voyager. The first-class lounge is one of the most elegant rooms on the ship. A smoking room (gents only) has a coal-burning fireplace (not to mention complimentary custom-made White Star matches). For the ladies, there is a reading and writing room with small writing tables that are nicely spaced and a glass enclosed bookcase that houses a lending library stocked with selections chosen by experts at the *London Times*.

For those craving a bit more activity, there's the promenade deck that allows first-class passengers to walk in the open air without having to bother going up on the boat deck. Or one can make use of the

APRIL 14, 1912

FIRST CLASS DINNER

HORS D'OEUVRES

OYSTERS

CONSOMMÉ OLGA

CREAM OF BARLEY

SALMON, MOUSSELINE SAUCE, CUCUMBER

FILET MIGNON LILI

SAUTÉ OF CHICKEN LYONNAISE

VEGETABLE MARROW FARCIE

LAMB, MINT SAUCE

ROAST DUCKLING, APPLESAUCE

SIRLOIN OF BEEF, CHATEAU POTATOES

GREEN PEAS

CREAMED CARROTS

BOILED RICE PARMENTIER & BOILED NEW POTATOES

PUNCH ROMAINE

ROAST SQUAB & CRESS

COLD ASPARAGUS VINAIGRETTE

PÂTÉ DE FOIE GRAS

CELERY

WALDORF PUDDING

The ship's gymnasium. Instructor T. W. McCawley demonstrates the rowing machine. The weight-lifting machine is to the right.

fully equipped gymnasium on the boat deck, which is the uppermost deck of the ship.

HOURS AS FOLLOWS:

10 A.M. TO 6 P.M.:
LADIES AND GENTLEMEN

1 P.M. TO 3 P.M.:
CHILDREN PERMITTED

THERE IS NO CHARGE FOR ADMISSION.

There are two bicycle racing machines that sit side by side so you can race a fellow passenger or yourself—the machines are connected to an oversized wall-mounted dial that will tell you your speed and distance, regardless of whether you want it to or not. There are two horse riding machines (one with an English sidesaddle for the ladies) that face each other, a rowing machine (which we thought rather ironic), clubs, a leather punching bag, an abdomen rubbing machine,

height and weight measuring devices—all of which are, of course, overseen by a professional.

In addition, there are squash racquets, a tiled Turkish bath where you can be spoiled by a masseuse, and, next to it, a heated, salt-water swimming bath!

The swimming bath has been improved even in the short time since October 1910, when the *Titanic*'s older sister took to the waves. The marble stairs, which had proved slippery, are augmented with helpful treads, and the springboards are nowhere to be found. It seems that on the *Olympic* they discovered that the water moved so much when they were at sea that the deep end frequently became the shallow end without the knowledge of some diving passengers. A springboard has not been installed aboard the *Titanic* in hopes of avoiding any further injuries.

Of course where first class on the *Titanic* truly shines is the accommodations. All of the first-class suites and rooms have the most up-to-date amenities such as hot and cold running water, and some even have coal-burning fireplaces. There are real beds, not berths, and windows, not portholes. There are even boards on the side of the bed that hinge down so as to form a little table for your morning cup of tea or to place your book on before nodding off.

two bedrooms, a sitting room, two wardrobe rooms, and a private bath and lavatory. Two have fifty-foot, glass-enclosed private promenades on the deck and cabins for the occupants' servants (provided at no extra cost).

First-class passengers aboard *Titanic* will have very little sense of being on a ship—

First-class stateroom B 59, decorated in the Old Dutch style (one of two beds shown).

dows, not portholes. There are even boards on the side of the bed that hinge down so as to form a little table for your morning cup of tea or to place your book on before nodding off.

The four fabulously expensive parlor suites are each decorated in a different period style and have as many as five rooms:

rather one feels embraced in a bejeweled, floating palace. Anything that might reveal reality is subtly camouflaged by the rare wood paneling, cascading drapery, shimmering silks, soft oriental carpet, glittering mirrors and more—all designed by Harland and Wolff's justifiably proud in-house decorators.

Welcome Aboard!

MADELEINE
FORCE
ASTOR

2597-2

ABOVE: American millionaire John Jacob Astor's young second wife, Madeleine.
RIGHT: Second-class passengers on the boat deck. Lifeboats with their deck gear can be seen at left.

★★★★★★★★★★★★★★★★★★★★★★★★★★★★★★★★★★★★

SAILING DAY!

TITANIC TAKES ON COAL, CREW, PROVISIONS, AND PASSENGERS

★★★★★★★★★★★★★★★★★★★★★★★★★★★★★★★★★★★★

MONDAY, APRIL 15, 1912

On Wednesday April 10, 1912, the *Titanic* began taking on coal, crew (officers and senior crew were already on board), provisions, and passengers, many of whom arrived by boat train from London.

The overwhelming majority of the 329 first-class passengers were American millionaires, with John Jacob Astor and his wife leading the luminous list. Mr. Astor, who sports a mustache and a military bearing, has added valuable Manhattan real estate (hotels and skyscrapers) to the fur trading

ASTOR, GUGGENHEIM, STRAUS—AMERICAN MILLIONAIRES IN FIRST CLASS

Astor and his airedale, Kitty, out for a walk on New York City's Fifth Avenue.

fortune he inherited and is now considered one of the wealthiest men in the world. His Newport, Rhode Island, garage houses his eighteen cars!

His airedale, Kitty, one of numerous canine traveling companions making the trip, also accompanies Mr. Astor. In addition, there is a Pekingese named Sun Yat Sen, a French bulldog named Gamon De Pycombe, a pomeranian, and a chow. Most will be residing in the ship's kennel and taken for daily walks by members of the ship's crew.

While in Egypt, the Astors met Mrs. James T. Brown, the estranged wife of a Denver, Colorado, gold mine owner. The unconventional (some say eccentric is too kind a word) Mrs. Brown is returning home to see her grandson, who is ill.

TITANIC ORCHESTRA

QUINTET PERFORMANCE TIMES AND LOCATIONS

ORCHESTRA LEADER: WALLACE HARTLEY

10:00 a.m. – 11:00 a.m.	After Second Class Entrance Foyer, C Deck
11:00 a.m. – 12:00 noon	First Class Entrance Hall, Boat Deck
4:00 p.m. – 5:00 p.m.	First Class Reception Room
5:00 p.m. – 6:00 p.m.	After Second Class Entrance Foyer, C Deck
8:00 p.m. – 9:15 p.m.	First Class Reception Room
9:15 p.m. – 10:15 p.m.	After Second Class Entrance Foyer, C Deck

Isidor Straus of Macy's Department
store in New York City, and his wife, Ida.

WHITE STAR'S ISMAY AND HARLAND AND WOLFF'S ANDREWS ON BOARD FOR MAIDEN VOYAGE

Isidor Straus, part owner of Macy's—the world's largest department store—is traveling with his wife of forty years. (On the rare occasions the two are separate they write each other daily.) Mining mogul Benjamin Guggenheim is yet another of the American millionaires making up the prestigious first-class passenger list, which includes only the fashionable, the worldly, and the well-known.

A first-class ticket on the *Titanic* is just the ticket for those who wish to see and be seen in today's fast-paced twentieth-century world. Indeed White Star's new luxury liner is not so much a mode of travel as a destination in herself.

White Star's proud-as-a-peacock chairman, Bruce Ismay, makes a point of accompanying each of his ships on their maiden voyages. Mr. Ismay was certainly not about to miss the *Titanic's* maiden voyage, perhaps the most important one in the company's long, illustrious history. Nattily attired, as always, he bid farewell to his wife and chil-

dren, who aren't going along (although his secretary and manservant will). Mr. Ismay will be staying in a deluxe suite on B deck.

Thomas Andrews, Harland and Wolff's managing director, has been on board since *Titanic's* recent successful trials. He is known to be devoted to all his ships, and this one in particular.

At noon the whistles blew signaling that friends, family, and well-wishers were required to depart so that the *Titanic* could.

Assisted by no less than six tugs, she approached the entrance to the harbor and was about to pass the *Oceanic*, which was moored side-by-side with the much smaller *New York* (both forced into idleness by the coal strike). However, the huge amount of water displaced by the *Titanic* caused the *New York* to unexpectedly move up and down, snapping the ropes binding her to the *Oceanic*. The thick ropes were flung toward the dock with such force that the crowd fled in near panic. (There were unconfirmed reports that a woman was injured and required medical treatment.) The unfettered *New York* began to veer ominously toward the *Titanic*, causing the captain of the smaller vessel to order mats thrown over the side to cushion the anticipated blow.

At the same time, a quick-thinking captain of one of the tugs, fearing his boat would be crushed between the two much larger vessels managed to get a wire rope around the *New York*, thereby slowing her down.

POTENTIALLY DANGEROUS COLLISION AVERTED

The *Titanic* aided her own cause by maneuvering to create a wave, which pushed the *New York* away. A potentially dangerous collision was avoided at the last moment.

It took the tugs an hour to negotiate the *New York* out of the way so that the *Titanic*, now behind schedule, could continue on her historic journey. The first port of call will be Cherbourg, France, and then on to Queenstown, Ireland, where the *Titanic* will take on mail and more passengers, including many Irish immigrants, heading for what they hope will be a better life in America.

Titanic is scheduled to arrive in New York's recently expanded pier 60 on the morning of April 17, 1912.

Bon Voyage!

SPECIAL NOTICE:

The attention of the managers has been called to the fact that certain persons, believed to be professional gamblers, are in the habit of traveling to and fro in Atlantic steamships.

In bringing this to the knowledge of travelers, the managers, while not wishing in the slightest degree to interfere with the freedom of action of the patrons of the White Star Line, desire to invite their assistance in discouraging games of chance, as being likely to afford these individuals special opportunities for taking unfair advantage of others.

Tugs taking the *Titanic* out to sea at Southampton. This photo was taken just before a near-collision with another, much smaller vessel.

MORE *TITANIC* STATISTICS

STAFF:

899 workers, including:

FIRST CLASS:

116 stewards

17 stewardesses

8 asst. pantryman stewards

6 plate stewards

5 asst. book stewards

16 bedroom stewards

5 linen stewards

SECOND CLASS:

45 stewards

3 asst. pantry stewards

4 plate stewards

3 boots stewards

12 bedroom stewards

THIRD CLASS:

45 stewards

4 glory hole stewards

GALLEY:

2 grill cooks

4 asst. vegetable cooks

4 asst. cooks

1 roast cook

1 Hebrew cook

6 asst. bakers

5 asst. butchers

4 kitchen porters

13 scullions

À LA CARTE RESTAURANT:

13 waiters

18 assistant waiters

1 wine butler

1 head waiter

1 chef

1 sauce cook

1 larder cook

1 entrée cook

1 roast cook

1 fish cook

1 pastry cook

carver

ice man

plate man

MISC.:

2 Marconi wireless operators

5 post office clerks

PROVISIONS:

75,000 lbs. fresh meat

11,000 lbs. fresh fish

25,000 lbs. fresh poultry and game

4,000 lbs. salted and dried fish

7,500 lbs. bacon and ham

2,500 lbs. sausages

40,000 fresh eggs

200 barrels flour

10,000 lbs. sugar

40 tons potatoes

3,500 lbs. onions

10,000 lbs. rice, dried beans

7,000 heads lettuce

5,500 lbs. tomatoes

2,250 lbs. fresh green peas

800 bundles fresh asparagus

36,000 oranges

16,000 lemons

2,200 lbs. coffee

800 lbs. tea

10,000 lbs. cereal

1,200 quarts fresh cream

1,750 quarts ice cream

1,000 sweetbreads

50 boxes grapefruit

1,000 lbs. hothouse grapes

1,500 gallons milk

600 gallons condensed milk

6,000 lbs. fresh butter

1,120 lbs. jam and marmalade

20,000 bottles of beer and ale

1,500 bottles of wine

15,000 bottles of mineral water

850 bottled spirits

CROCKERY:

57,000 pieces, including:

   12,000 dinner plates

   2,500 breakfast plates

   3,000 teacups

   1,500 soufflé dishes

GLASSWARE:

29,000 pieces, including:

   8,000 cut tumblers

   2,500 water bottles

   2,000 wine glasses

   3,000 claret jugs

CUTLERY:

44,000 pieces, including:

   8,000 dinner forks

   2,000 egg spoons

   1,000 oyster forks

LINEN:

196,100 items

Thursday, April 11, 1912, 8:30 a.m.

The seas have been calm, and the weather has been clear,
if somewhat crisp, since we left Southampton; some of
my fellow passengers take brisk walks on the boat deck
to work up an appetite before the eight o'clock bugle
announces breakfast; others stay in their cabins to read
a fresh copy of the <u>Atlantic Monthly</u>, the ship's newspaper
(one of the many privileges of first class).

In the afternoon, most passengers take advantage
of the chairs on the boat deck and sit, bundled up in
steamer rugs, talking to each other or writing letters,
keeping journals, reading, or just relaxing with a hot cup
of broth. Some of the braver souls throw quoits or play
shuffleboard, tennis, or cricket (nets prevent the balls
from going overboard).

Various groups make it their habit to pass the time
playing cards (bridge, whist, poker, patience, etc.) or
dominoes in the smoking room. Others prefer the solitary
indoor pleasure of reading quietly in the library. (Frankly,
my favorite activity is sampling the fare at each of the
outstanding eating establishments onboard.)

Another popular activity seems to be sending and
receiving Marconi wireless messages (Marconigrams is the
proper term). Most of my fellow passengers treat it like a

new toy and play with it endlessly, sending Marconigrams
to family, friends, business associates, and, I suspect,
perfect strangers; mostly about the most trivial of matters.
But no matter, the Titanic has two full-time wireless
operators whose sole responsibility (they work directly for
Mr. Marconi, not White Star--indeed they don't technically
even report to the captain) is satisfying the passengers'
whims. The Titanic, of course, has the most modern radio
equipment available.

Evenings are spent in the smoking room discussing
politics, business, and a rather wide variety of
miscellaneous topics in exhaustive detail. Most recently
it's been the astonishing number of honeymooners on board
(30); apparently the lure of sailing on the Titanic's maiden
voyage is too much for newlyweds to resist.

Junior wireless operator Harold Bride sending and receiving
messages in the *Titanic's* Marconi room.

The *Titanic* at Cherbourg, France, at dusk, April 10, 1912. Additional passengers boarded here.

Friday, April 12, 1912, 4:30 p.m.

John Jacob Astor and Hudson Allison joined us last night.
I found Mr. Astor to be a surprisingly stimulating and
unconventional personage. Mr. Allison is an exceedingly
wealthy Montreal businessman. Mrs. Allison and the family--
Loraine, age 2, and Trevor, age 11 mos.--are traveling
with them. I had the pleasure of meeting Loraine yesterday
in the Verandah Café, which has become a favorite with
the first-class children. They are accompanied by the
children's nanny and nurse, who are in adjoining cabins,
and their cook and chauffeur who are in second class.

Col. Gracie (who is Teddy Roosevelt's cousin) certainly
attracts the most attractive women on board and has been
gracious enough to introduce us to them. The aptly named
Mrs. Helen Candee, who is divorced with two children, is
going to America to see her son, who has been seriously
injured in an airplane accident.

Col. Gracie is also responsible for introducing me to
Mr. and Mrs. Straus. (The Col. and Mr. Straus can be spotted
walking the promenade deck, deep in discussion, on a daily
basis.) I spent a wonderful afternoon Friday talking with
Mr. Straus of Macy's and so much more. After a while Mrs.

Straus joined us. She is herself
involved in numerous charitable
affairs. They are, by any
measure, an extraordinary couple:
born on the same date, four
years apart--imagine that! And
married now nearly forty years.
They are a welcome reminder that
the institution of marriage, which
we all know is being threatened
from all sides today, still holds
a sacred place in our society, and
that love and devotion are not
just words from a bygone era.

I've made a number of
acquaintances on my own. One
most fortunate encounter was
with Major Arthur Peuchen,
another wealthy Canadian
businessman, a most interesting
chap who is also the vice-
commodore of the Toronto yacht
club (he proudly reported).

I've even managed to meet
some people in second class.
Miss Edwina Troutt, with two
T's, who insists you call her
Winnie, has certainly gotten
around. She crossed the Atlantic
the first time when her friends
said she didn't have the nerve.
She has been a clerk in a
tobacco store, a waitress, and
a domestic. She's returning to
Massachusetts to assist her
pregnant sister.

Amateur military historian
Col. Archibald Gracie.

Helen Candee, a dynamic and highly
independent American author who wrote
How Women May Earn a Living.

Saturday, April 13, 1912, 5:00 p.m.

For Thomas Andrews, the <u>Titanic</u>'s designer, this clearly is no pleasure cruise. He patrols the ship daily, dressed in his work clothes--a rather rough-looking boiler suit affair--and is followed attentively by his eight eager assistants. Andrews scrutinizes every square inch of the <u>Titanic</u> like the proud but concerned parent he is. His eagle eye is constantly on the lookout for any deficiency he can remedy: no detail is too small. I inquired what, precisely, he had found, and he allowed me to have a look at the notebook he keeps close at hand at all times:

*too many screws in the stateroom hat rack   *paneling too dark in first-class staterooms   *tile too light in various places
*check ladder leading up to berths   *check malfunctioning kitchen fan
*check inefficient hot press   *check heat in second-class staterooms

Even Andrews, however, doesn't work as hard as the <u>Titanic</u> staff, the majority of whom are involved in the running of the grand hotel part of the ship, not the sea-going part. They work from dawn to dusk (and before and after) to ensure that passengers are guaranteed every comfort. They clean and sweep out the public rooms before any of us are up, wash down the deck, make the beds, endlessly clear, set, and reset the numerous tables in the numerous restaurants and cafés, while unseen, down below, the firemen toil ceaselessly feeding the furnaces that keep the <u>Titanic</u> steaming along.

Andrews and I had breakfast this morning, and he inquired if I would mind accompanying him to his room, as he had to review some documents before he headed off on his self-appointed rounds. His room was filled to overflowing with blueprints in various states of unravel, heaps of surveys threatening to topple over at a moment's notice, and what appears to be a lifetime supply of diagrams, all of which cover any available surfaces. Mr. Andrews is clearly a man who takes his responsibilities seriously. He confers daily with White Star Chairman J. Bruce Ismay, who occupies one of the fabulous parlor suites.

Mr. Ismay is preoccupied with charting the <u>Titanic</u>'s progress and is pleased to see that the speed is improving each day:

Day one: 464 miles   19.3 knots average speed
Day two: 519 miles   21.6 knots
Day three: 546 miles   22.8 knots

Harland and Wolff's managing director, Thomas Andrews. He oversaw the design and construction of the *Titanic*.

Sunday, April 14, 1912, 10:30 p.m.

The Sunday inspection took place as scheduled but the lifeboat drill did not. The drill was to have included crewmembers in lifejackets stationed at their assigned boats as well as passengers (who are not assigned boats). The consensus is that the captain considers the boat unsinkable and the drill, therefore, wholly unnecessary.

Mr. Ismay made it crystal clear to Captain Smith that the ship is to arrive in New York city a day ahead of schedule. He is so confident that he has already placed an ad in the New York Times announcing that we will dock on Tuesday, not Wednesday (as previously stated). He is most eager, apparently, to reap all of the rewards that will surely be forthcoming when the magnificent vessel dramatically and triumphantly arrives in America earlier than anticipated.

The "no cards on Sunday" rule has been waived, which is a relief to any number of my fellow passengers. The rumor is that there are more sharks onboard than below and caution is the watchword. Since I never participate in games of chance, I shan't concern myself any further.

There has been some talk about wireless messages from other ships warning of icebergs in our path. There were supposedly two on Friday and one on Saturday. In fact a French liner has collided with an iceberg, and the captain has wisely taken the precaution of altering our route to a more southerly arc; Captain Smith has our full confidence.

The news engendered a lively and, I must say, most informed discussion over lunch where I learned everything there is to know about "bergs" (which is what one calls them while at sea). The average age of an iceberg is 3,000 years. One is formed when warm weather causes a glacier to calve a huge chunk of ice into the ocean. They can vary greatly in size, the largest being virtually indestructible;

Some of the lifeboats on the *Titanic*. Originally 32 were planned, but that number was reduced to 16.

the smaller ones are called "growlers" although no one seems to know why. 7/8ths of an iceberg is underwater, and when they come together it is called an ice pack.

One woman, whose name I didn't catch, said you can smell them before you can see them. Apparently spotting one at night is particularly difficult. The woman, who was quite learned on the subject, went on to say that one way to spot a "berg" on a windy night is from the white foam that appears when the ocean's swell meets the "berg's" base. Since the sea right now is so still, that could be a problem. She said it's even worse if it has its "black" side facing us. It seems that icebergs can melt, change shape, turn over, and absorb seawater so that they are no longer completely white but blue/gray and therefore even harder to see than their all-white brethren. Icebergs, she stated matter-of-factly, were an inconvenience, not a danger. This

Captain Smith (front row, second from right) and his officers. First Officer William Murdoch sits to the right of Smith. Second Officer Lightoller is in the back row, second from left.

latter remark seemed to annoy the gentleman on her left, who had been silent up to now.

He informed us, sotto voice and quite off the record, that he overheard a conversation between Second Officer Lightoller and one of the crewmen (Lightoller's status as first officer was reduced when Captain Smith made last-minute changes). The binoculars used by the lookouts, which are supposed to be kept in the crow's nest (90 feet straight up and reached by an absolutely dizzying spiral staircase located inside the forward mast), are missing. It seems that Second Officer Lightoller was aware of the situation but unable to locate them. According to our informant, Lightoller explained to the crewman that, depending on the conditions, you can see an iceberg just as easily with the naked eye.

This sparked a rather lively debate between the gentleman and the woman. The final straw for her was when he said that the crow's nest was not considered by everyone to be the best place from which to spot icebergs. The perspective, he explained (accompanied by sketches he was now making), from that height allowed the "berg" to blend in with the surroundings and virtually disappear. The best place for a lookout to be was down at the waterline, he stated with a particularly self-satisfied manner. The woman asked him where on earth he had heard that, and he shot back, "Antarctic explorer Ernest Shackleton," which put an end to the conversation.

All agreed iceberg sightings were quite common this time of year.

Ran into Mr. Astor at the barbershop--he too was there for his daily shave. We discussed the fascinating array of articles available there. Not only pens, combs, toothbrushes, wallets, chewing gum, and chocolate, but an equally extensive selection of trinkets with the Titanic name on them--flags, plates, spoons, ribbons, miniature life rings--all of which can be bought as a memento of the voyage.

There's a daily sweepstakes and everyone places bets on the ship's speed that day. Reportedly we are now moving along at a rather brisk 22 knots. The resulting wind accentuates the cold; the temperature has dropped to 33 degrees--only one degree above freezing. You can feel the ship speeding up; the vibrations from the engines are stronger. There is talk that Monday we are going to increase our speed so we can see just what the ship can do. Col. Gracie informed me that Captain Smith assured him we would arrive in New York ahead of schedule.

Had dinner in the à la carte restaurant and saw Mr. Ismay, who was dining as usual with the ship's doctor. Col. Gracie informed me that he intends to play squash and then go for a swim in the morning, so we postponed our breakfast date an hour.

Ran into Second Officer Lightoller, who had finished his rounds and was on his way to bed, which seems to be everyone's destination. Mrs. James J. Brown, who is also known as Margaret, uncharacteristically said she was exhausted and was going to read before turning in. I decided to head for the smoking room to see if I can drum up some excitement. I could hear music and what sounded like hysterical screaming emanating from the third-class common room on D deck. Clearly a good time is not confined to the first or second class.

Denver's wealthy and flamboyant Margaret Brown.

11:45 p.m.

The engines have stopped running. The ship's forward motion continues but she is definitely slowing down; the breeze that comes through the open portholes has subsided considerably.

The conversation in the smoking room has also subsided. All of us are wondering why the captain has chosen to stop in the middle of the ocean at midnight. We are, naturally, curious, but no one is alarmed.

Apparently we have struck an iceberg!

We can hear alarm bells, which means that they are closing the watertight doors; merely a precaution, I am sure.

Some of the passengers felt a slight jar; one described the sound as being like the ship was running over a thousand marbles. The chief night baker said he knew something was wrong when the pan of rolls he had just baked fell off the top of the oven and scattered all over the floor. A crewman who was down below, much closer to the point of impact, said it sounded like steel being ripped open; a gross exaggeration no doubt. If the contact with the iceberg had been at all serious there would have been a sudden, shocking jolt and we would have all been sent flying, which is far from the case.

People are ringing for their stewards and poking their heads out of their staterooms seeking information. Some were awakened by the sound of ice falling through the portholes. The children down in steerage are playing with ice chunks, and a snowball fight is scheduled for the morning.

Apparently we were very close to the iceberg when it was spotted. Damage, however, is minimal and there is no danger. We will soon be on our way.

12:02 a.m.

The collision has resulted in more damage than was initially thought. The iceberg has torn a gash in the Titanic's hull and water is pouring in. Andrews found that six of the watertight compartments have been breached. The mailroom is flooded and the postal clerks are attempting to save the two hundred bags of mail that are floating in two feet of water, all the while hurriedly removing the letters from the cubicles. The pumps will not be able to stem the tide. Andrews has informed the captain and Mr. Ismay that the <u>Titanic</u> has only a short time--hours--before she sinks to the bottom of the ocean.

Needless to say this is most incredible.

Edith Evans stoically told Col. Gracie and me that a fortuneteller in London had warned her to beware of the water--the implication was clear to both of us. We tried to assure her that all would turn out all right in the end but our words sounded rather hollow. Despite this, Miss Evans is exceedingly calm.

The purser's office on C deck is inundated with people who want, understandably, to withdraw their valuables. There is a bit of confusion; some of the stewards are telling their passengers that there is nothing to worry about while others go around politely knocking on stateroom doors and advising everyone to put on lifejackets and go up to the boat deck. Some are not so polite--there are reports of stateroom doors being forced open as the inhabitants were still sleeping. Many of them are angry about being disturbed at this late hour and have returned to bed.

John Jacob Astor.

MRS. JOHN JACOB ASTOR

The captain has
ordered the lifeboats
uncovered . . .

Passengers are
to put on their
life jackets and
come up to the boat
deck. Some of the
passengers feel this
is most unnecessary
and are not wearing
them, a position I
find inadvisable.
Col. Gracie has half-
jokingly cancelled
his squash game
tomorrow morning.

Mr. and Mrs.
Astor have donned
their life jackets
and are sitting,
motionless, on the

Madeleine Astor.

mechanical horses in the gymnasium. Mrs. Astor is dressed,
as usual, to the nines: including her diamond necklace and
ever-present muff. Mr. Astor has cut open one of the life
preservers to show her what is inside.

People are walking around the boat deck in various
stages of dress and dishevelment: some wear evening gowns
with coats casually thrown over their shoulders, while
others are in hastily tied kimonos and bathrobes. One woman
is wearing her evening slippers sans stockings. Arthur
Peuchen has shed his evening attire and put on two sets

of long woolen underwear and several warm layers on top of that. Benjamin Guggenheim is wearing a warm sweater over his life jacket--something his steward has insisted on. Mrs. Brown has on her long, black velvet dress (the one with the satin trim) and her long, black velvet coat. She is carrying her warmest stole, just in case.

The unspoken words on everyone's lips are: "Is this really happening?"

12:45 a.m.

There was just an explosion--brilliant white stars bursting hundreds of feet in the air directly over the ship, followed by a shower of sparks: distress rockets. This can only mean one thing: we are in danger and are calling for help from any ships in the area.

The crewmen are taking the canvas covers off the lifeboats, clearing the lines and fitting the cranks off the davits (the mechanisms that lower the boats). There are sixteen lifeboats (numbered 1-16), eight on each side, and four collapsible boats (A, B, C, D) that have canvas covers that can be pulled up when in use.

The officers and crew seem unfamiliar with the davits and confused about what the proper procedures are; all of which complicates the matter considerably and wastes time. Time that I am coming to believe we do not have. The officers are afraid if they fully load the lifeboats, the davits will not hold, the boats might flip over in midair, or they will capsize when they meet the sea. The lifeboats are being loaded with much confusion and very little sense of urgency. The instructions are that the women and children are to be loaded first (someone suggested that the honeymoon couples go first but the grooms declined).

The officers are having a difficult time convincing the women to enter the boats. Some are simply afraid to leave the Titanic and step into a lifeboat that is dangling precariously seventy-five feet over the ocean and sways madly while it is being lowered. Most of them do not believe the situation is dire enough to warrant going out

One of sixteen wooden lifeboats dangling from the lifting hooks and lowering gear that launched the boats. Captain Smith watches from the bridge.

on a cold night on the unimaginably vast ocean where the
water temperature is 28 degrees. They feel they will be
safer aboard the <u>Titanic</u> where they can wait in comfort
until one of the ships in the area takes us off. (Supposedly
one of these ships is steaming toward us at this very
moment--although I have heard no official confirmation of
this.) There are heart-wrenching scenes as men kiss their
wives good-bye while assuring them there is no danger, that
this is just a precaution. Many fathers are bidding farewell
to their children, patting them on the head like they are
sending them off for their first day of school, their faces
gallantly transformed into masks of fearlessness.

The lifeboats are leaving less than half full. The
disorderly and confusing situation is further complicated
by the decision to let some of the men (passengers and
crew) climb aboard if there are no women available in the
immediate area. Many of the men are reluctant--but not all.
Some of the boats have left without enough seamen to man
them and do the rowing, while others lack provisions like
water, sailing equipment, and essential implements like
knives.

Some stewards are locking the stateroom doors after
they have ensured that the occupants are out, as a precaution
against looters.

The chief baker and his staff have made bread, which
they are distributing into the lifeboats.

Captain Smith appears indecisive. There seems to be no
overall plan or strategy.

The ship's orchestra has assembled in the first-class
lounge and is playing, which has a most desirous calming
effect. Groups of men and women stand around and talk;
laughter, at times, erupts into the night air. Combined

The *Titanic*'s orchestra. Pictured from top left: Fred Clarke, Percy C. Taylor, G. Krins, Wallace Hartley (Bandmaster), W. T. Brailey, Jock Hume, J. W. Woodward. Not pictured: Roger Bricoux

with the music, it appears as if we are at a slightly bizarre but still quite gay party in the middle of the Atlantic Ocean.

Andrews said the chief engineer is committed to keeping the power going as long as possible so that the lights remain on and the wireless distress signals can continue to be sent. Coolheaded, as always, he seems to be everywhere, helping everyone. He instructed one of the stewardesses to make sure all the passengers have put on warm clothes and are making their way up to the boat deck, and that all the spare rooms were open and the life belts and blankets in them were distributed. The stewardess said she was reluctant to put on her life belt because she didn't want to convey the wrong message to the passengers. Andrews assured her that it was better she set a proper example and added that if she wanted to live she should put it on. Now he is either urging women and children to get into the boats or helping them board.

1:00 a.m.

Lightoller is loading lifeboat #6 and Mrs. Straus started to get in but then changed her mind and stepped back. She insists that she will not leave her husband: "We have been living together for many years; where you go I go," she told him. Col. Gracie tried to convince Mrs. Straus to change her mind but she would not hear of it. The Col. then suggested that Mr. Straus could get into the lifeboat with her (due, I presume, to his advanced age). He too refused, saying he would not go before the other men.

Mrs. Straus then helped her maid, Ellen Bird, into the boat and gave Miss Bird her fur coat saying she would need it. "Wear this, it will be cold in the lifeboat, and I do not need it anymore."

Mrs. Straus waved a handkerchief as the lifeboat rowed away, and then she and her husband sat down on the deck chairs.

Astor asked Lightoller if he could accompany his wife into the lifeboat because of her "delicate condition": he refused the request. Astor bowed out like a gentleman, asking the second officer the lifeboat's number so he could meet her in the morning.

The Titanic sits calmly in the still water, her lights, which continue to burn brightly, reflecting off the placid surface, casting a glow all around us, as if we were being blessed from above. This is hardly the case, however. The sky is star-filled and moonless. I have never seen, read, or imagined anything so eerie and otherworldly.

Mr. and Mrs. Allison are quite concerned, to put it mildly; they don't know where Trevor, their youngest son, is. He was last seen with the nanny. Mrs. Allison, who is nearly hysterical, refuses to board a lifeboat until she has found him. The crew attempted to place Loraine in one but Mrs. Allison won't allow it, gathering Loraine up in one of her skirts to protect her from the cold.

1:30 a.m.

Benjamin Guggenheim has reappeared. Gone is the warm sweater and lifebelt, replaced by white tie and tails. He told the steward: "I think there is grave doubt that the men will get off. I am willing to remain and play the man's game if there are not enough boats

Benjamin Guggenheim, a soft-spoken, but steely American millionaire.

for more than the women and children. I won't die here like a beast. Tell my wife . . . if it should happen that my secretary and I both go down and you are saved, tell her I played the game out straight and to the end. No woman shall be left aboard this ship because Ben Guggenheim was a coward."

Some of the officers were stopping young boys from entering lifeboats. In one case Astor jammed a young girl's hat on one of the boy's head and pushed him into the boat.

There are only six lifeboats left.

Ismay is helping the women into the lifeboats. When a stewardess said she didn't think she should get in because she was only a stewardess he told her that being a woman was all that mattered. Recently, however, he appears to be in a state of panic. He patrols the deck wearing an overcoat thrown over his pajamas and slippers, frantically barking out ineffectual and incomprehensible orders to the crewmen, who don't know who he is and are too busy to care.

Ismay was helping to load collapsible C, and just as the boat was being lowered, and seeing that there were no women in the immediate vicinity, he quietly climbed over the side and slid in.

The women and children have been called up from third class. I thought all the women had been placed in lifeboats, but apparently not. It seems they remained down there all this time, patiently waiting for instructions. I understand that when they were finally summoned they had great difficulty negotiating their way through the entirely unfamiliar passageways that led up to the boat deck where the lifeboats are. There are rumors that some of the crewmen locked the passageways because they feared the steerage people would overrun the lifeboats and cause

Lifeboat #6 with Margaret Brown and Helen Candee on board.

a riot. They have all their belongings in bags hoisted over their shoulders or carried under their arms. It is impossible to understand what they are saying, because they do not speak English. They can see that nearly all the lifeboats are gone. There are also rumors that some of the men have donned women's clothing and are attempting to sneak onto the remaining boats. The situation is getting out of control.

A man with a heavy Middle Eastern accent came running up to Edwina Troutt clutching an infant in his arms. He frantically told her he didn't want to be saved but would she take his nephew, which she did, getting into boat 16.

Another foreigner brought his two young boys wrapped in a warm blanket and, after saying something to them, placed them in collapsible D.

Col. Gracie escorted Miss Evans and Mrs. Brown to collapsible D, which appears to be the last boat. There was only one seat left and Miss Evans insisted Mrs. Brown take it, saying, "You go first. You have children waiting for you."

I am going to accompany Mr. Astor down to the kennels. He wants to free Kitty and the other dogs. It seems only fair they should have a fighting chance.

When I returned to the smoking room, Thomas Andrews was standing there with his arms crossed, staring either at the fireplace or at the painting above it. He took no notice of my presence, and I was loath to disturb his reverie. A steward came in and saw Andrews's lifebelt lying on a nearby table. "Aren't you even going to try for it, Mr. Andrews?" he said. Andrews didn't move or say anything, only continuing to stare straight ahead.

2:00 a.m.

The ship's orchestra has put on their lifebelts and has moved to the boat deck near the entrance to the grand staircase.

The boiler room crew has come up on deck. The chief engineer and his men remain down below.

Captain Smith is on the bridge. He told the crew it's every man for himself. Some are simply jumping overboard, while others continue to throw deck chairs and any wooden objects that might float into the sea in hopes that they might be of use.

Megaphone in hand, the captain reminds the lifeboats to be sure to return to pick up those of us who are washed into the ocean once the ship goes down. He is not wearing a lifebelt.

The ship's lights are no longer burning brightly but glowing an ominous red. She is going down by the head. The stern is rising higher and higher. You can hear the crashing as anything that isn't bolted down--tables, chairs, sofas, bureaus, glasses, dishes--is sliding faster toward the bow. Water is coming right up to the deck and people are panicking, pushing, moving back toward the stern and keeping away from the rails.

It's t

LEFT: A photograph of the *Titanic* taken by a family traveling only from Southampton to Queenstown.

EDITOR'S NOTE: How Vanni's unique journal survived is a story in itself. Apparently Vanni cut a piece of tarp, wrapped it tightly around his journal, and then taped it to his chest. He dove into the sea and swam frantically until he happened upon a bundle of deck chairs that one of the crewmen had roped together and thrown overboard precisely for this purpose. Vanni was then taken aboard one of the lifeboats. He was delirious, nearly unconscious, and suffering from hypothermia (the temperature of the water was 28 degrees). Summoning what little strength he had left, Vanni kept pointing to his chest; those on the lifeboat assumed he had injured something and was in pain. He kept gesturing until he died only an hour before the rescue ship *Carpathia* arrived on the scene. His somewhat waterlogged but salvageable journal was removed and preserved. This is the first time it has appeared, and it is presented unedited.

THE *TITANIC* HOUR BY HOUR

MONDAY, APRIL 22, 1912

9:00–11:00 A.M. SUNDAY, APRIL 14: *Wireless messages received reporting ice directly in the* Titanic's *path. Messages posted on ship's bridge.*

1:42 P.M.: *Another wireless warning of ice. Captain Smith gives message to Ismay, who puts it in his pocket; message not posted on bridge.*

7:15 P.M.: *Smith asks Ismay to give him back the message; it is then posted on bridge.*

7:30 P.M.: *Jack Phillips, the* Titanic's *senior wireless operator, hears warning from nearby* Californian—*ice only fifty miles away, straight ahead.*

8:55 PM: *Smith returns to bridge after dinner; discusses weather, calm seas with Second Officer Lightoller.*

9:20 P.M.: *Smith returns to cabin.*

9:40 P.M.: *Another wireless warning; Phillips, overwhelmed by outgoing messages coming down the pneumatic tubes, places it under paperweight and forgets about it.*

ABOVE: The *Titanic's* wireless operators: Twenty-five-year-old senior operator Jack Phillips (top) and twenty-one-year-old junior operator Harold Bride. RIGHT: Seventeen-year-old John Thayer jumped feet first as the ship went down. Later that day he described the collision while a passenger on the rescue ship sketched.

Strikes Starboard Bow - 12¹ A.M.   11²⁵ P.M.

Forward End Floats,   1.⁵⁰ A.M.
Then Sinks

Settles by Head - Boats Ordered Out   12.⁰⁵ A.M.

Stern Section Pivots Amidships and Swings over Spot where Forward Section Sank.   2.⁰⁰ A.M.

Settles to Forward Stack Breaks Between Stacks   1.⁴⁰ A.M.

Last Position in which "Titanic" Stayed 5 minutes Before the Final Plunge

L.P. Skidmore, S.S. "Carpathia" Apr. 15ᵗʰ 1912.

10:00 P.M.: *Frederick Fleet and Reginald Lee take over as lookouts; Lightoller's previous order to be alert for icebergs is passed on.*

10:30 P.M.: *The* Rappahonnock, *eastbound and emerging from an ice field, warns the* Titanic *via signal lamp.* Titanic *replies: "Message received. Thanks. Good night." No changes are made.*

10:55 P.M.: *Another message from the* Californian; *they are surrounded by ice (the same field as* Rappahonnock). *Phillips tells the* Californian *to "shut up." Messages thus far describe a pack of ice 78 miles wide directly in* Titanic's *path. The* Californian *shuts down her wireless transmitter. She neither sends nor receives messages and is the ship closest to the* Titanic.

11:40 P.M.: *Lookout Frederic Fleet sees an object, a black mass, in the haze; small at first, it grows as the* Titanic *bears down on it. Fleet rings crow's nest bell three times, picks up phone, and reports to bridge: "Iceberg right ahead."*

Officer on bridge thanks Fleet, repeats warning to first officer. First officer pulls switch that closes the watertight doors to the boiler and engine rooms; attempts to maneuver ship in an S-shaped pattern, hoping to avoid collision. The maneuver fails, and the Titanic *runs into the submerged portion of an iceberg weighing, possibly, half a million tons.*

11:45 P.M.: *Andrews, summoned by Smith, arrives at bridge, assesses damage, and reports that ship has only hours before she sinks. Ismay arrives and is informed of the situation.*

11:55 P.M.: *Harold Bride, who was asleep, arrives to relieve Phillips who tells Bride the ship has been injured and they may have to return to Belfast for repairs. Phillips is heading for bed when Smith arrives and orders him to send a distress signal. Bride insists he use the Morse code call SOS, joking that it might be Phillips's last chance. The SOS from the* Titanic *was one of the first British uses of the universal distress signal. Created in 1905, the three dots, three dashes, three dots are so easy even amateurs can send it. (SOS does not stand for anything.)*

MIDNIGHT: *Smith orders lifeboats uncovered.*

12:25 A.M., MONDAY, APRIL 15: *The* Titanic's *officers see lights of a nearby ship 5 miles away and signal, unsuccessfully, on Morse lamp.*

The Carpathia, *which missed the first distress calls, contacts the* Titanic, *which replies: "Come at once. We have struck a berg and require immediate assistance." The* Carpathia *says she is 58 miles away and "coming hard."*

Captain orders an increase in speed, change of course, and the firing of signal rockets at fifteen minute intervals.

12:45 A.M.: *First lifeboat (#7) is lowered. First distress rockets fired.*

1:27 A.M.: *The* Titanic *transmits message: "We are putting off the women in the boats."*

1:40 A.M.: *Collapsible C with Ismay onboard is lowered. Last distress rockets fired.*

2:05 A.M.: *Collapsible D, last boat, is lowered.*

2:10 A.M.: *Smith relieves wireless operators, who remain, transmitting the distress signal.*

2:17 A.M.: *Ship's orchestra is forced to stop playing due to slant of deck.*

2:18 A.M.: *Lights go out.*

2:20 A.M.: *Ship sinks.*

3:05 A.M.: *Sounds of people struggling in the water cease.*

3:35 A.M.: *The* Carpathia's *rockets are sighted by lifeboats.*

4:10 A.M.: *First lifeboat (#2) taken aboard the* Carpathia.

5:15 A.M.: *The* Californian, *released by the ice, gets under way; heads for the* Titanic's *position.*

8:00 A.M.: *The* Californian *arrives in area of sinking.*

8:30 A.M.: *Last lifeboat (#12) taken aboard the* Carpathia.

8:50 A.M.: *The* Carpathia *heads for New York.*

A wide expanse of ice and, possibly, the iceberg that sank the *Titanic*. This photo
was taken by a passenger on the rescue ship *Carpathia*, Monday, April 15, 1912.

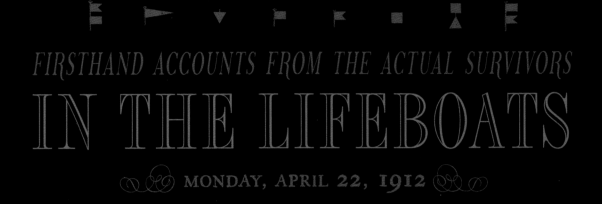

FIRSTHAND ACCOUNTS FROM THE ACTUAL SURVIVORS
IN THE LIFEBOATS
MONDAY, APRIL 22, 1912

The absolute calm of the sea, while it militated against the detection of the iceberg in our path, at the same time made it possible for all the lifeboats lowered from the davits to make their long and dangerous descent to the water without being smashed against the sides of the ship, or swamped by the waves breaking against them.

Col. Archibald Gracie,
Washington, D.C.
First Class
Collapsible B

As our lifeboat number 13 pulled out from the side of the *Titanic* we could see the water rushing into the ship. Rowing away, looking at the *Titanic*, it was a beautiful sight outlined against the starry sky, every porthole and saloon blazing with light. It was impossible to think anything could be wrong with such an enormous ship, were it not for the tilt downwards towards the bow. . . . Finally as the *Titanic* sank faster, the lights in the cabins and saloons died out. At the same time the machinery roared down through the vessel with a rattle and a groaning that could be heard for miles— the weirdest sound, surely, that could be heard in the middle of the ocean, a thousand miles from land.

It was not until the *Titanic* went down with all those people on the decks— screaming and jumping into the water— that I realized the seriousness of it. My mother, brother, and sister had been put in a lifeboat before I was, so I knew they had gotten off the ship.

It was impossible to think anything could be wrong with such an enormous ship, were it not for the tilt downwards towards the bow. . . .

All lifeboats were supposed to be equipped with oars, a compass, a light, and food (crackers). Our lifeboat had only oars. The other boats seemed to be in the same predicament because we were all scattered. But we were very lucky. The captain of the boat said he had been at sea for 26 years and he had never seen such a calm night on the Atlantic.

Miss Ruth Elizabeth Becker, 12,
India and Benton Harbor, Michigan
Second Class
Lifeboat #13

The boat we were in started to take in water; I do not know how. We had to bail. I was standing in ice-cold water up to the top

---

I was standing in ice-cold water up to the top of my boots all the time, and rowing continuously for nearly five hours.

---

of my boots all the time, and rowing continuously for nearly five hours. We took off about fifteen people who were standing on a capsized boat. In all, our boat had by that time sixty-five or sixty-six people. There was no room to sit down on our boat, so we all stood, except some sitting along the side.

Mrs. John Borland Thayer,
Haverford, Pennsylvania
First Class
Lifeboat #4

The men who were rowing our boat were stokers. They had been working near the bottom of the ship near the boilers when the *Titanic* struck. Therefore, when the ship was ripped open, the water rushed in and soaked all of them. They escaped with nothing on except sleeveless shirts

Some of the last surviving passengers to be taken aboard the *Carpathia*.

Titanic survivors recovering aboard the *Carpathia*.

and shorts. So you can imagine how cold they were out in that freezing weather. The officer in charge asked me to give up my blankets to wrap around these men, which I gladly did.

And then with all of this there fell on the ear the most terrible noises that human beings ever listened to—the cries of hundreds of people struggling in the icy cold water, crying for help with a cry that we knew could not be answered. We wanted to pick up some of those swimming, but this would have meant swamping our boat and further loss of lives of all of us.

Ruth Becker

The men with the paddles, forward and aft, so steered the boat as to avoid contact with the unfortunate swimmers pointed out struggling in the water. I heard the constant explanation made as we passed men swimming in the wreckage, "Hold on to what you have, old boy; one more of you aboard would sink us all." In no instance,

If they had turned back several hundred more would have been saved. No one can explain it.

I am happy to say, did I hear any word of rebuke uttered by a swimmer because of refusal to grant assistance. . . . There was one transcendent piece of heroism that will remain fixed in my memory as the most sublime and coolest exhibition of courage and cheerful resignation to fate and fearlessness of death. This was when a reluctant refusal of assistance met with the rigning [*sic*] response in the deep manly voice of a powerful man, who, in his extremity replied: "All right, boys; good luck and God bless you."

. . . there arose to the sky the most horrible sounds ever heard by mortal man except by those of us who survived this terrible tragedy. The agonizing cries of death from over a thousand throats, the wails and groans of the suffering, the shrieks of the terror-stricken and the awful gaspings for breath of those in the last throes of drowning, none of us will ever forget to our dying day. "Help! Help! Boat ahoy! Boat ahoy!" "My God! My God!" were the heart-rending cries and shrieks of men, which floated to us over the surface of the dark waters continuously for the next hour, but as time went on, growing weaker and weaker until they died out entirely.

Col. Archibald Gracie

The most heart-rending part of the whole tragedy was the failure, right after the *Titanic* sunk, of those boats, which were only partially loaded, to pick up the poor souls in the water. There they were, only four or five hundred yards away, listening to the cries, and still they did not come back. If they had turned back several hundred more would have been saved. No one can explain it.

John Thayer
Haverford, Pennsylvania
First Class, Collapsible B

Two French boys, ages two and three, who were crossing with their father.

Twelve-year-old second-class passenger Ruth Becker, who was separated from her family but survived (as did they).

The cries, which were loud and numerous at first, died away gradually one by one, but the night was clear, frosty and still, the water smooth, and the sounds must have carried on its level surface free from any obstruction for miles, certainly much farther from the ship than we were situated. I think the last of them must have been heard nearly forty minutes after the *Titanic* sank. Lifebelts would keep the survivors afloat for hours; but the cold water was what stopped the cries.

Lawrence Beesley,

London, England

Second Class

Lifeboat #13

Swings were lowered to take us up. I was the first one to be put into the swing and tied in because I was so numb I couldn't hold on.

We all, of course, were watching for the light of a rescue ship. Finally about 4 o'clock in the morning we did see a light, which came closer and closer. Rockets were being sent up and the foghorn kept blowing and blowing.

You can imagine our joy because we knew it must be a rescue ship. All of us shouted and yelled. We were really happy because the sea was getting choppy and that was the first time I was a little concerned. Our tiny boat bounced around like a cork. The *Carpathia*, our rescue ship, stopped. We rowed to it, and our boat load was rescued.

Swings were lowered to take us up. I was the first one to be put into the swing and tied in because I was so numb I couldn't hold on. I was pulled up to the top and taken into the waiting room where the survivors were given brandy and hot coffee. Blankets were piled to the ceiling. I thawed out immediately without the brandy and coffee.

Around 10 o'clock I found my mother. A passenger came to me and said, "Are you Ruth Becker?" I said, "Yes." She said, "Your mother's been looking all over for you."

Ruth Becker

"CAPTAIN COURAGEOUS"

AN EXCLUSIVE MODERN TIMES INTERVIEW WITH THE CAPTAIN OF THE CARPATHIA

MONDAY, APRIL 29, 1912

ARTHUR H. ROSTRON, a highly respected, twenty-seven-year seaman, was given command of the *Carpathia* only three months ago. His fellow mariners know him as "Electric Spark" because of his high-level intensity and ability to take decisive action under pressure. A God-fearing man, the captain does not smoke, drink, or curse. He graciously agreed to tell us about his ship's role in the recent tragedy at sea.

MODERN TIMES: You and your ship sailed from New York on April 11 bound for Liverpool and the Mediterranean, correct?
CAPTAIN ROSTRON: Yes, most of our passengers were American tourists or third-class immigrants who were returning to their country of birth for a visit.

MT: When were you first made aware of the *Titanic*'s situation?

CAPT. A. H. ROSTRON — UNDER OFFICERS "CARPATHIA"

CR: We were three days out of New York, and at 12:25 a.m. Monday, April 15, my wireless operator received a transmission from the *Titanic*. He entered my cabin without knocking, which was a sure sign that the news he brought was both dire and urgent. When he told me about the transmission I asked him, twice, if he was certain it was the *Titanic* and he said he was.

MT: I take it you asked twice because you thought it extraordinary that the *Titanic* should need help.

CR: Correct.

MT: Did you respond to the wireless from the *Titanic*?

CR: Yes, I told them we were coming as quickly as possible and expected to be there within four hours.

MT: How far away were you?

CR: 58 miles southeast of the *Titanic*'s position.

MT: What did you do then?

CR: I immediately turned the ship around and told the chief engineer I wanted maximum speed. All heat and hot water to the passengers was to be cut off so that it could be diverted to the engines. Off-duty crewmen were ordered to return to their stations and extra lookouts were posted on the bow and the crow's nest to watch for ice. I instructed them to look for the reflection of starlight off the iceberg, as the sea was too calm to hope for ripples around the berg's base.

MT: How bad was the ice?

CR: There were twenty-five to fifty large bergs in the area and hundreds of smaller ones.

MT: Please continue.

CR: Lights were strung alongside the ship, gangways were readied, and slings and canvas bags were put in place. All public rooms and any unoccupied cabins were also readied to accommodate the survivors. First-aid stations were set up in the three dining saloons with a surgeon assigned to each and tea, coffee, soup, and food were prepared.

MT: What time did you finally arrive in the area that the *Titanic* had last transmitted as her position?

CR: At 3:35 a.m., I began firing rockets at fifteen-minute intervals so that if there were any lifeboats they could see us. At 4:00 a.m., I saw a green light, and that was the first lifeboat.

MT: And that's when you began taking survivors onboard?

CR: Yes.

MT: How did you learn that the *Titanic* had sunk?

CR: I asked one of the *Titanic*'s surviving officers where the ship was and he said, "Gone! She sank at 2:20 a.m.!" I then asked him how many were onboard when she went down and he said hundreds and hundreds. Although I had feared the worst because we hadn't had a transmission from the *Titanic* for hours, I was still stunned.

MT: Was it difficult getting everyone onboard?

CR: Most of the men were able to climb up the ladders. The women were taken up in slings, while the children and injured were brought up in canvas bags.

MT: What were your more than 740 passengers doing while this was taking place?

CR: Most of them were gathered along the railing and were silently and solemnly watching the painful process that was taking place below them. They had collected extra clothing and gathered toiletries, such as toothbrushes. The barbershop had contributed hairpins. The ship's officers and all the male passengers and many of our women passengers gave up their cabins, and our

The *Carpathia* in her New York dock. She is being reprovisioned and refueled so she can continue her journey.

steerage passengers were grouped together to make room for the *Titanic*'s steerage people. The survivors were taken into the dining saloons where they were served hot tea, coffee, and soup and a sandwich.

MT: Can you tell me something about their condition?

CR: Medically speaking they were suffering from frostbite and hypothermia, which was to be expected. Mentally speaking, I think they were overwhelmed and trying to wake up from the nightmare they had been in for the last four hours, and some were trying to grapple with the realization that they had lost their husbands and loved ones. I must say that they were extraordinarily calm and orderly, especially considering the circumstances. Everyone behaved magnificently.

MT: We understand you held a funeral service that night.

CR: Yes, its purpose was twofold: a remembrance for those unfortunate souls who did not survive and a time to give thanks for those who did survive.

MT: Where did the survivors sleep?

CR: All over; on the floor in the saloons, the library or the smoking room—anywhere they could make themselves comfortable. I think they just wanted to rest from the ordeal and recover their strength as fast as possible.

MT: White Star chairman J. Bruce Ismay, we now know, was one of the few first-class males who survived. Can you tell us something about his condition at the time?

CR: Mr. Ismay was, I believe, mentally very ill when we took him in. I immediately decided to assign him to the ship's doctor's cabin where he was heavily sedated.

MT: Did you discuss the situation?

CR: Only briefly. I suggested he send a message to New York and he agreed, sending: "Deeply regret advise you *Titanic* sank this morning after collision iceberg, resulting serious loss of life. Full particulars later."

MT: We understand that the junior wireless operator, Harold Bride, also survived.

CR: Yes, he was suffering from frostbite and badly injured feet.

MT: Apparently Mr. Bride was one of the fortunate men—we understand there might have been as many as thirty—who were saved by hanging on to the collapsible boat that had overturned as soon as it was washed off into the ocean.

CR: Yes, that is correct.

MT: Jack Phillips, the senior wireless operator, was, we learned, unable to hold on and therefore perished.

CR: That appears to be so.

MT: Some are already comparing Jack Phillips and Harold Bride to Jack Binns, the heroic wireless operator aboard the *Republic* who remained at his post three years ago when his ship was rammed in thick fog off the coast of Nantucket. Binns, as I am sure you know, not only repaired the damaged equipment but continued to send out distress signals for thirty-six consecutive hours while enduring freezing cold, wet, and exhaustion. He is credited with saving the lives of the 750 passengers onboard and became an instant American hero.

CR: Well, I am not in the business of anointing heroes; I can only say what I know of first-hand and that is that Mr. Bride was most helpful to us. Our wireless operator was himself exhausted from the night's activities and I was committed to transmitting the names of the survivors as well as their messages. Mr. Bride agreed to lend a hand even though he was suffering greatly. Indeed, due to his injuries he had to be carried to the wireless room.

MT: Is it true that three of the *Titanic's* survivors were the nieces of two of your passengers?

CR: Yes, in fact they had sent a wireless greeting from the *Titanic* only the day before. The aunt and uncle slept through the ordeal and had no idea what was happening until they were informed by a steward that their nieces wanted to see them.

MT: Who made the decision to bring the survivors to New York?

CR: I did.

MT: From the time you learned of the *Titanic* disaster until you arrived in New York you refused to respond to any inquiries, including one from the President of the United States. Was that also your decision?

CR: Yes. My main concern, besides getting to New York safely, of course, was transmitting messages from the survivors. Inquiries from the press were of no interest to me. As far as the president's query is concerned I was not made aware of it at the time.

Harold Bride being carried off the *Carpathia*. His bandaged feet are frostbitten. Senior wireless operator Jack Phillips did not survive.

140447

MT: As you know, nature abhors a vacuum, but not nearly as much as the press does. Your radio silence during this critical time resulted in a great deal of speculation and rumor. Of course the story was carried in every major newspaper in America and, with the noteworthy exception of the *New York Times*, they were all reporting that the *Titanic* was safe, that she was being towed to Halifax, and that all passengers had been transferred to other ships that had responded immediately to her calls for help. In fact, White Star, due to delays in transmission, had not received Chairman Ismay's telegram. A company vice president issued a statement that said: "We are absolutely satisfied that even if [the *Titanic*] was in a collision with an iceberg she is in no danger. With her numerous water-tight compartments she is absolutely unsinkable, and it makes no difference what she hit. The report should not cause any serious anxiety."

CR: I was unaware of all of this and rather had my hands full with the matter at hand. My priority, indeed my only priority, was getting our passengers and the survivors of the *Titanic* to a safe harbor. Until that mission had been accomplished to my satisfaction I did not think it proper or appropriate to devote time or energy to other matters.

MT: Was the voyage to New York a smooth one?

CR: As I said earlier, there were numerous icebergs, and the weather was most uncooperative: bitterly cold winds, storms, and choppy seas all the way.

MT: Could you describe for our readers the situation you encountered when you entered New York harbor on the night of April 18?

CR: We on the *Carpathia* had no way of knowing about the extraordinary response to the sinking. My ship was immediately surrounded by veritable flotilla: ferries, tugs, yachts, boats of various shapes and

Three first-class passengers (right) who survived in lifeboat 5.

sizes. The decks of the tugs—and there must have been at least fifty of them—were filled with newsmen shouting out questions or offering up money to the survivors watching from the railing, through these megaphones that they all seemed to have. Meanwhile, the photographers were shooting off their magnesium flashbulbs in the darkness of the night. This, combined with the rain and lightning, only added to the otherworldly nature of the scene.

MT: You were not aware that a crowd of over 30,000 was surrounding the pier being barely controlled by nearly every policeman in New York?
CR: No.

MT: And, of course, that would mean you didn't know that many in the crowd were

friends and family of the survivors who were only going to learn if their loved ones were alive when you docked?
CR: That's correct; we knew nothing about any of this.

MT: Did you or your officers speak to any of the reporters?
CR: No.

MT: Your first stop was not, as expected, the Cunard pier to unload your precious cargo. Why not?
CR: First we went to the White Star pier because I wanted to unload the *Titanic's* lifeboats, which we had brought back with us. After that we headed for the Cunard pier, where by 9:30 p.m. we began disembarking our own passengers first and then the survivors from the *Titanic.*

• A CLOSING NOTE FROM THE PUBLISHER •

There were 1,324 passengers on the *Titanic* and 899 crew for a total of 2,223.

1,517 died and 706 survived.

685 crew members perished.

40% of the passengers in first class, 58% in second, and 75% in third class did not survive.

Nearly all of them were frozen to death.

CAPTAIN SMITH and *Titanic's* designer Thomas Andrews went down with the ship, as did Andrews's assistants. The chief engineer and all engine room officers died. Although the chief engineer released his thirty-five men some time before 2:00 a.m., they remained at their posts keeping the electricity and the lights operating until the last minute.

THE EIGHT MUSICIANS in the ship's orchestra continued to play until the very last and lost their lives. All of the restaurant staff but one; the five postal clerks; and every page, lift, and messenger boy perished. None of them even attempted to get into a lifeboat.

WHITE STAR CHAIRMAN J. BRUCE ISMAY climbed into collapsible lifeboat C and literally never looked back. Bent over his oars he never turned around to see his ship sink beneath the sea.

He was criticized by both the American and British inquiries that were held immediately after the tragedy (more severely by the former). The American press vilified him and held him accountable. Rear Admiral A. T. Mahan, a widely respected naval historian, wrote: "I hold that under the conditions, so long as there was a soul that could be saved, the obligation that lay upon Mr. Ismay was that the one person and not he should have been in the boat."

Ismay was pictured in a cartoon cowering in the lifeboat with the name "J. Brute Ismay" affixed.

Ismay had apparently believed the media

Bruce Ismay, whose survival remains one of the major controversies surrounding the sinking of the *Titanic*.

that were calling the ship "unsinkable." The original designer of the *Titanic*, Alexander Carlisle, recommended that she be equipped with forty-eight lifeboats; Ismay reduced that number to thirty-two. Later, looking to increase the number of first-class cabins, the amount of promenade space, and overall profits, he further reduced the number to just sixteen.

"We spent two hours discussing carpet for the First Class cabins and fifteen minutes discussing lifeboats," Carlisle stated after the sinking.

The sixteen lifeboats actually met, and even slightly exceeded, the outdated, unrealistic British Board of Trade regulations. In fact, nearly all ships at the time routinely shorted

MODERN TIMES: YOUR WORLD, ILLUSTRATED ❧ SPECIAL EDITION

lifeboat numbers. The *Titanic* had lifeboats for 962 people maximum, even though the ship's capacity was 3,000.

The *Titanic* could remain afloat if up to four of her sixteen watertight compartments flooded. Six were flooded in the early morning hours of April 15, 1912.

Ismay's decision to cut back on lifeboats doomed hundreds to a watery grave.

He retired from White Star and withdrew from the business world. He attended no social functions and saw only family and friends. From time to time he took walks in London's parks or went to concerts by himself (buying an extra seat for his hat and coat). During the two investigations he bought a remote retreat in Ireland, site unseen, and spent a great deal of time there shooting and fishing.

His wife would not allow the subject to be brought up, and she stated numerous times that the *Titanic* had ruined their lives.

SECOND OFFICER CHARLES LIGHTOLLER'S survival was nothing short of miraculous. He escaped from the sinking ship at the very last moment, dove into the sea, was nearly sucked under as the ship went down, but was blown clear. Lightoller was able to grab a rope that was dangling from collapsible boat B, which had been washed from the deck and was now overturned in the sea. Lightoller was one of twenty-eight men hanging on to the boat.

Ismay (at head of table, hand to face) being questioned during the U.S. Senate investigation.

Second Officer Lightoller (with pipe) and Third Officer Herbert Pitman in Liverpool, England, after testifying at the U.S. hearings.

He was the very last person taken aboard the *Carpathia*.

Charles Lightoller was the principle witness at both hearings, and defended his actions as well as Ismay's, Captain Smith's, and the other officers'. He performed admirably, answering hundreds of questions. He was scornful of the proceedings and said they "make our seamen, quartermasters and petty officers look ridiculous." Clearly Lightoller believed what he said: "A washing of dirty linen would help no one." He defended the decision to proceed at full speed through a known ice field as standard operating procedure and concluded that there was "an extraordinary combination of circumstance that existed at the time, a combination that would not happen again in a hundred years. It is extraordinary that they

should have existed on this particular night; everything was against us, everything."

He was forever after associated with Ismay's ignominy, and White Star never gave him a command of his own. Lightoller served in World War I and then retired. During World War II he and his son sailed their sixty-foot yacht during the incredible British rescue effort at Dunkirk. Despite being unarmed and attacked by German airplanes, thanks to Lightoller's sailing ability they made it back with 131 soldiers.

LOOKOUT FREDERICK FLEET, who first spotted the iceberg, was ostracized by senior British naval officers during his twenty-four more years at sea because of his testimony during the hearings. He said that he would have spotted the iceberg earlier if he had his binoculars, blaming his senior officers by implication. (Unbeknownst to anyone on the *Titanic* at the time, the binoculars were on the ship in a locker belonging to an officer who was transferred at the last minute.) Evidence at those same hearings indicated that Fleet may have had trouble judging distance, a curious drawback for a lookout on a ship speeding through the ice-infested waters of the North Atlantic at night.

Eventually Fleet became a night watchman and later sold newspapers on the streets of his hometown, Southampton, England. Over the years he suffered from depression, and two weeks after his wife died he became despondent and wrote: "I am in deep trouble I have just lost my wife, also I am leaving my house the place where I have been living their [*sic*] is only my brother-in-law and myself and we cannot agree."

Two days later, Fleet committed suicide by hanging himself in the garden of his brother-in-law's house.

CAPTAIN ARTHUR ROSTRON of the *Carpathia* was given an American Congressional Medal of Honor and went on to have a distinguished career.

IN 1977 DR. ROBERT BALLARD of the Woods Hole Oceanographic Institution began his quest to discover the precise location of the *Titanic* on the ocean floor. Others had tried and failed, but on September 1, 1985, the joint American/French operation that Dr. Ballard headed located the wreck, ten miles from where she was thought to have gone down. A year later Dr. Ballard and his team began undersea exploration of the wreck, which was 2.5 miles below the surface. The successful mission provided otherworldly films of the ship and much information. For one thing, the investigation showed that once the stern had risen up, the ship broke in two before sinking. Perhaps even more important, it showed that there are six narrow slits where the plates had parted—not a gash caused by the iceberg tearing through the iron hull as originally thought. The wreckage suggests that the rivets popped along the seams, allowing water to rush in, causing the liner to sink as rapidly as it did.

HARLAND AND WOLFF'S decision to build the *Olympic* and *Titanic* simultaneously may have played an important role in the sinking of the latter, according to allegations made in 2009 by two materials scientists. They claim that the shipbuilder encountered serious difficulty in finding skilled riveters and high-quality rivets, a problem that peaked during the construction of the *Titanic*. They were then forced to settle for substandard wrought-iron rivets that were used on the central hull and bow—precisely where Dr. Ballard's exploration shows the *Titanic* was struck by the iceberg that forced her to the bottom of the ocean.

The two scientists subjected forty-eight rivets recovered from the wreck to computerized modern failure analysis. The results suggest that if proper steel rivets had been used the ship might have remained afloat longer, allowing nearby ships to rescue hundreds more passengers.

Harland and Wolff, long silent on the subject, has recently rejected these allegations.

A WORD FROM THE AUTHOR

ONCE WHEN I WAS EIGHT my grandparents took me to one of my favorite places: the library. That particular weekend I chose Bruce Catton's book *A Stillness at Appomattox* and began to read it as soon as we got back to my grandparents' Brooklyn apartment. I remember that book as if I read it yesterday. At times I felt truly transported, as if I was there with Generals Grant and Lee.

Fast forward to the present—now *I* write books on subjects like the Civil War. But times have changed. We no longer process information the way we did just a short time ago. Not remotely. The array of information tools we have access to is dazzling. Our factoid, sound byte–oriented news comes from bulletins, blogs, and crawls that creep across room-sized flat screens that feature hi-def and 3-D. D as in dimensions, like depth. To get information about difficult and complex concepts, we Google, download and scan, or listen to podcasts. This technologically driven paradigm shift is both a challenge and an opportunity for an author; especially an author of books for young readers. Confronting and considering it I was inspired to conceive *Titanic Sinks!*'s bold, unconventional, and multifaceted approach to the tragedy. My objective is to remove the distorting curtain of time and eliminate the dubious benefits of hindsight to make history come alive, to create a sense of being there.

The *Modern Times* magazine format allows me to present a great deal of information in a variety of visually dramatic ways: headlines, subheads, articles (all meticulously researched and written by me); first-person accounts (the "In the Lifeboats" section is composed entirely of the testimony of actual survivors); photographs, ads, posters, statistics, menus, and memorabilia.

For an intimate perspective on the critical events of April 10 to 15, I allowed the fictional chief correspondent of *Modern Times*, S. F. Vanni, to accompany the great ship on her maiden voyage. All information, and indeed all observations and conversations in this section, are scrupulously based on extensive research. Only Vanni is invented. Unlike the authors of virtually all other books on the subject, I decided to use photographs of the *Titanic* exclusively. There are no photographs of her nearly identical sister ship, the *Olympic*, in *Titanic Sinks!* The *Titanic*, of course, was not around long enough to be photographed extensively. She was built, launched, and sank before anyone had time to take many pictures. It was tempting to use the many photographs of the *Olympic*—especially those of her interior. However, I felt it would detract from the historically accurate and eerie tone I was trying to create.

SURVIVOR JOHN THAYER came to believe that the *Titanic*'s sinking was "The event which not only made the world rub its eyes and awake, but woke it with a start."

An "event" that poses many questions, none more important than this: Does something that happened so long ago have any meaning, now that the world is so vastly different? I agree with acclaimed filmmaker James Cameron, director of the award-winning epic movie *Titanic*, who suggests "that basic human nature was the same in 1912. . . . Cover-up lies, corporate denial of guilt or responsibility, these are not new concepts."

In 1912 many believed that the *Titanic*'s fate was the result of man's folly. He had greatly exaggerated his power and come to worship all things technological. Technology would solve all of society's ills. A century later, in 2011, that blind faith in technology sound eerily familiar. Perhaps *Titanic Sinks!* will serve as a timely reminder that man's inclination to arrogance and power must always be balanced by humility and perspective. For, as Bob Dylan warns:

Praise be to Nero's Neptune
The *Titanic* sails at dawn.
And everybody's shouting
"Which side are you on?"

The promenade deck, photographed during the Southampton to Queenstown portion of the fateful maiden voyage. (The man walking away is often identified as Captain Smith but, alas, isn't.)

PHOTO CREDITS

© Bettmann/CORBIS, pp. 36, 43 · Cork Examiner/Southampton City Heritage Collections, p. 10 · Daily Graphic, p. 14 · The Daily Mirror/Mirrorpix Photo Archives, p. 9 · Don Lynch Collection, p. 56 · editorial recreations, pp. 15 bottom, 20 bottom, 22 top · Encyclopedia Titanica, p. 27 top · The Father Browne Photographic Collection, p. 12 · Father Browne/Universal Images Group/Getty Images, p. 3 · George Grantham Bain Collection/Library of Congress, pp. 18, 34, 37, 54, 55, 57, 58, 59, 63 · © Hulton-Deutsch collection/CORBIS, pp. i, 31 · © Illustrated London News Ltd/Mary Evans, pp. 8, 19, 41 · Library of Congress Prints and Photographs Division, pp. 50-51, 62, 65 · Mary Evans/The National Archives, London, England, p. 29 · Mary Evans/Onslow Auctions Limited, p. 13 · Mary Evans Picture Library, p. 26 · © National Museums Northern Ireland 2011, Collection Harland & Wolff, Ulster Folk & Transport Museum, pp. i-iii, 2, 5, 7, 11, 17, 32 · © National Museums Northern Ireland 2011, Ulster Folk & Transport Museum, pp. iv-v, vi-vii, 67 · New York World-Telegram and the Sun Newspaper Photograph Collection/Library of Congress, pp. 20 top, 46, 53 · © Schenectady Museum; Hall of Electrical History Foundation/CORBIS, p. 3 · Science & Society Picture Library/Getty Images, p. 49 · Strauss Historical Society, p. 21 · Topical Press Agency/Stringer/Hulton Archive/Getty Images, p. 66 · The U.S. National Archives/ARC Identifier 278337/ ML Number 383, p. 45 · Universal Images Group/Getty Images, pp. viii, 15 top, 16, 22 bottom, 25, 48 top, 48 bottom, 64, 69 · Wikipedia, from the collection of Randy Bryan Bigham, p. 27 bottom

Every effort has been made to contact and acknowledge rights holders for all images. We apologize for any unintentional errors o

SOURCE NOTES

"a fancy-dress ball . . .": Butler, *"Unsinkable,"* 89.

"Luxury and comfort . . .": author construct.

"British know-how backed . . .": author construct.

"As always, superior . . .": author construct.

"practically unsinkable": McCarty, *What Really Sank the Titanic*, 21.

"a technological miracle . . .": author construct.

"the Millionaire's Captain . . .": Lynch, *Titanic*, 35.

"I cannot imagine . . .": McCarty, *What Really Sank the Titanic*, 12.

"Don't you bother . . .": Marcus, *Maiden Voyage*, 82.

"lunatic, idiot": Beveridge, *Titanic* Vol. Two, 25.

"Hours as follows . . .": Beveridge, *Titanic*, Vol. Two, 204

"*Titanic* orchestra . . .": Beveridge, *Titanic*, Vol. Two, 27.

"Special notice . . .": Beveridge, *Titanic,* Vol. Two, 35.

"Too many screws . . .": author construct.

"We have been . . .": Butler, *"Unsinkable,"* 109.

"Wear this . . .": Davie, *Titanic*, 49.

"I think there is . . .": Butler, *"Unsinkable,"* 123.

"You go first . . .": Butler, *"Unsinkable,"* 130.

"Aren't you even . . .": Butler, *"Unsinkable,"* 132.

"Message received . . .": Marcus, *Maiden Voyage*, 127.

"Iceberg right ahead . . .": Lynch, *Titanic*, 85.

"Come at once" and "Coming hard": Butler, *"Unsinkable,"* 98.

"We are putting . . .": Eaton, *Titanic: Destination Disaster*, 72.

"shut up.": Butler, *"Unsinkable,"* 66.

"The absolute calm . . .": Gracie, *Titanic*, 62.

"As our lifeboat . . .": Eaton, *Titanic: Destination Disaster*, 35.

"It was not . . .": Eaton, *Titanic: Destination Disaster*, 41.

"All lifeboats . . .": Eaton, *Titanic: Destination Disaster*, 35.

"The boat we were in . . .": Gracie, *Titanic*, 45.

"The men who were . . .": Eaton, *Titanic: Destination Disaster*, 35.

"The men with the paddles . . .": Gracie, *Titanic*, 60.

"there arose . . .": Gracie, *Titanic*, 48.

"the most heart-rending . . .": Davie, *Titanic*, 79.

"The cries . . .": Beesley, *The Loss of the S.S. Titanic*, 60.

"We all, of course . . .": Eaton, *Titanic: Destination Disaster*, 36.

"Swings were lowered . . .": Eaton, *Titanic: Destination Disaster*, 42.

"Gone!": Marcus, *Maiden Voyage*, 186.

"Deeply regret . . .": Marcus, *Maiden Voyage*, 187.

"We are absolutely . . .": Brinnin, *The Sway of the Grand Saloon*, 374.

"There were 1,324 passengers . . .": U.S. Senate Inquiry.

"I hold . . .": Marcus, *Maiden Voyage*, 205.

"We spent . . .": Butler, *"Unsinkable,"* 99

"make our seamen . . .": Davie, *Titanic*, 182.

"a washing of . . .": Marcus, *Maiden Voyage*, 222.

"extraordinary combination . . .": Marcus, *Maiden Voyage*, 256.

"I am in deep trouble . . .": Davie, *Titanic*, 41.

"The event which not only . . .": Davie, *Titanic*, xvi.

"that basic human nature . . .": Kuntz, *Titanic Disaster Hearings*, xii.

BIBLIOGRAPHY

Archbold, Rick, and Dana McCauley. *Last Dinner on the Titanic.* Toronto: The Madison Press Limited, 1997.

Baker, Roy Ward. *A Night to Remember.* Janus Films, 1958.

Beesley, Lawrence. *The Loss of the S.S. Titanic: Its Story and Its Lessons.* Charleston: Forgotten Books, 1912.

Beveridge, Bruce, and Scott Andrews. *Titanic: The Ship Magnificent;* Volume One: *Design & Construction.* Stroud, Gloucestershire: History Press Limited, 2008.

Beveridge, Bruce, and Scott Andrews. *Titanic: The Ship Magnificent;* Volume Two: *Interior Design & Fitting Out.* Stroud, Gloucestershire: History Press Limited, 2008.

Biel, Steven. *Down with the Old Canoe: A Cultural History of the Titanic Disaster.* New York: W. W. Norton & Company, 1965.

Brinnin, John Malcolm. *The Sway of the Grand Saloon: A Social History of the North Atlantic.* London: Macmillan London Unlimited, 1972.

Brown, David G. *The Last Log of the Titanic.* Camden, Maine: International Marine/Ragged Mountain Press, 2001.

Bullock, Shan F. *"A Titanic Hero": Thomas Andrews, Shipbuilder.* Mattituck, New York: Amereon Limited, 1996.

Butler, Daniel Allen. *"Unsinkable": The Full Story of the RMS Titanic.* Cambridge, Massachusetts: Da Capo Press, 1998.

Davie, Michael. *Titanic: The Death and Life of a Legend.* New York: Alfred A. Knopf, Inc., 1986.

Eaton, John P., and Charles A. Haas. *Titanic: Destination Disaster; The Legends and the Reality.* New York: W. W. Norton & Company, 1987.

Eaton, John P., and Charles A. Haas. *Titanic: A Journey Through Time.* New York: W. W. Norton & Company, 1999.

Eaton, John P., and Charles A. Haas. *Titanic: Triumph and Tragedy.* Second edition. New York: W. W. Norton & Company, 1994.

Geller, Judith B. *Titanic: Women and Children First*. New York: W. W. Norton & Company, 1998.

Gracie, Col. Archibald. *Titanic: A Survivor's Story*. Stroud, Gloucestershire: Sutton Publishing Limited, 1985.

Hyslop, Donald, and Alastair Forsyth. *Titanic Voices: Memories from the Fateful Voyage*. New York: St. Martin's Press, 1999.

Kultur Video. *Titanic: Born in Belfast*. VHS, 2001.

Kuntz, Tom, editor. *The Titanic Disaster Hearings: The Official Transcripts of the 1912 Senate Investigation*. New York: Simon & Schuster, 1998.

Lord, Walter. *A Night to Remember*. New York: Bantam Books, 1955.

Lynch, Don. *Titanic: An Illustrated History*. Edison, New Jersey: Wellfleet Press, 2006.

McCarty, Jennifer Hooper, and Tim Foecke. *What Really Sank the Titanic: New Forensic Discoveries*. New York: Citadel Press Books, 2008.

Marcus, Geoffrey. *The Maiden Voyage*. Norwalk, Connecticut: The Easton Press, 1969.

Marshall, Logan. *Sinking of the Titanic and Great Sea Disasters*. New York: Quill Pen Classics, 2008.

New York Times, *The Tragic Voyage: Times Coverage of the R.M.S. Titanic*. New York: The New York Times, 2009.

Noxon, Nicolas. *Secrets of the Titanic*. DVD. National Geographic, 1999.

Peltier, Melissa. *Titanic: The Complete Story*. DVD. A&E Home Video, 1994.

Quinn, Paul J. *Titanic at Two A.M.: Final Events Surrounding the Doomed Liner*. Sacco, Maine: Fantail, 1997.

Reade, Leslie. *The Ship That Stood Still: The Californian and Her Mysterious Role in the Titanic Disaster*. New York: W. W. Norton & Company, 1993.

United States Senate Inquiry, April 17, 1912. www.titanicinquiry.org.

Wade, Wyn Craig. *The Titanic: End of a Dream; The Complete, Definitive Story From the Doomed Voyage to the Spectacular Discovery of the Wreckage*. New York: Penguin Books, 1979.